# Technical Communication for Information Managers

# Technical Communication for Information Managers

*By*
Prof.(Dr) G. Devarajan

Ess Ess Publications
New Delhi

***Technical Communication for Information Managers***



**ISBN: 978-81-7000-671-8**

**Rs.525/-**

**First Published 2012**

Published by:
**Ess Ess Publications**
4831/24, Ansari Road,
Darya Ganj,
New Delhi-110 002.
INDIA
Phones: 23260807, 41563444
Fax: 41563334
E-mail: info@essessreference.com
www.essessreference.com

Cover Design by *Patch Creative Unit*

Printed and bound in India at Salasar Imaging Systems.

# Contents

# PREFACE

Technical communication is a method of researching and creating information about technical processes or products directed to an audience through media. Technical communicators often work collaboratively to create products for various media, including printed media, video and the Internet. Technical communication sometimes considered as a professional task for which organisations either hire specialised employees or outsource their needs to communication firms. The process of developing information products in technical communication begins by ensuring that the nature of the audience and their need for information is clearly identified. As the information product is created, the paramount goal is ensuring the audience's needs in the most appropriate format. Technical communication is important to professionals who are engaged in various types of information activities including information management especially in the present day ICT environment. This book is focused on varied aspects of technical communication and how various types of information products are generated with a theoretical and practical perspective.

The book is organised under eight chapters. Chapter one deals with Communication- communication process and types of communication . Technical communication- characteristics of technical communication , various categories of technical writings are given in chapter two. Chapter three outlines the language as a medium of communication. In chapter four reader-writer relationship and readability and text are given. Chapter five provides various aberrations in technical writing. In chapter six is given how information is organised in various technical documents such as abstract, technical article, thesis, project proposals etc. Chapter seven deals with information consolidation and repackaging while chapter eight contains an account of editor, editing, editorials tools and proof reading . A comprehensive bibliography is also given as adjunct to for further reading and research

This book has been intended for the library and information science students and teachers, practicing professionals in libraries and information centres who are engaged in the various types of information activities including information management in particular and scientific community in general. The author records his appreciation and profound thanks to Mr. Sumit Sethi, M/S Ess Ess Publications, New Delhi for brining out this book in good format within record time.

Trivandrum **Prof.(Dr) G.Devarajan**

# 1

# Communication

## 1. INTRODUCTION

Communication is obviously fundamental to any kind of social activity. It is therefore a topic of study by a very wide range of disciplines in Science and technology, social sciences and humanities. It is the indispensable activity of mankind and ends with the last breath. In scope, communication is so vast and covers language, para-language, body language, signs, symbols of both the animate and the inanimate.

### 1.1. What is Communication?

The word communication originated from the Latin root of 'communicare' and 'communis' which means to share, and this sharing is of information, knowledge and thought. It is essentially an art by which a person shares knowledge, feelings, ideas, information etc in a way that each gains a common understanding of the meaning, intent and use of the message.

Communication may be defined as:

- act or instance of transmitting
- imparting or interchange of thoughts, opinions or information by speech, writing etc;
- something imparted, interchanged or transmitted;
- document or message imparting information, opinion, etc;

- process by which information is exchanged between individuals or groups through a common system of symbols.

An analysis of the above definitions can be reduced to two basic components such as process of communication and the message communicated. The study of communication typically involves both elements. The above statements also imply that for information to be transmitted, it has to be first mentally conceived, generated or formed by an individual; only then can the information be communicated to another. The transmission process, could , however be oral, through visual images or through written text in any language; or a combination of all these different modes of communication. As a matter of fact, seventy percent of man's active life is spent in communication and involves in all activities like reading, writing, listening, speaking, scolding, criticising, conversing, singing, praising, arguing, instructing, pleading, justifying, living, hating, comprehending, opposing, soothing and healing.

## 1.1. Communication Process

The elements involved in a successful communication process are the 'communicator' or source, ' Message' or information, 'Channel' or transmitter and 'Communicatee' or target. In fact communicator is the element which may be an entity i.e person or document which generates the element message or information that is passed through the channels or transmitter such as verbal or non-verbal and is received the message by the communicatee or target or recipient as represented below.

Communicator → Message → Channel → Communicatee.

## 1.2. Communication Models

There are mathematical models to illustrate the flow of information from the communicator to the communicatee in the communication process. Harold D Lasswell's verbal model which became known as Lasswell Formula was: 'Who says What in Which Channel to Whom with What Effect'

Who → Says What → In Which Channel→To Whom→With What Effect
(Sender) (Message) (Medium) (Receiver) (Impact)

The above formula denotes Who is the sender or communicator; Says what is Message or information ; in which channel is Medium; to whom is the Receiver or recipient and With what effect is impact or feedback. The transmission of the receiver's response to the sender is called feedback.

***The Shannon – Weaver model.***

The publication by Shannon and Weaver in 1949 has become a classic, and has influenced thinking about communication across most of the disciplines involved. The model is represented below.

Information source → Message → Transmitter → Signal → Noise → Received signal → Receiver → Message → Destination.

The Shannon- Weaver model represents communication as a linear flow process . This is obviously a partial reflection of how communication works. In the communication process the signal can be distorted by interfering 'noise' which means that the signal received by the receiver is not necessarily identical to the one sent by the transmitter.

In brief, the essentials of effective communication are:

- A common communication environment;
- Cooperation between the sender and the receiver;
- Selection of an appropriate channel
- Correct encoding and decoding of the message;
- Receipt of the desired response and feedback.

## 1.3. Objectives of communication

The objectives of communication may be stated as :

i) to facilitate effective decision making;

ii) to develop information and understanding required for effective teamwork;

iii) to attain high productivity and higher job satisfaction;

iv) to form positive attitudes required for motivation, action, cooperation, coordination etc;

v) to help people understand the need for a change and to reduce the resistance to change.

### 1.4. Seven C's of successful communication

The principles or parameters applied for effective messages are known as seven C's of communication as stated below.

- correctness
- Completeness
- Consciousness
- Clarity
- Creativeness
- Courtesy
- Consideration

Correctness means that there is no mistake of grammar, punctuation and spellings. It should be grammatically correct. All information should be accurate and timely. If our message or document is not of good level of correctness then it has no effect on receiver and it may cause difficulties. So the objective of communication will be failed.

Completeness implies that our message should include all necessary facts and background information. It should include everything the reader needs for the reaction we desire. We must include all information which our receiver wants. If our message is not complete to bring desirable results then the receiver will not be convinced by us.

Conciseness means to convey information in fewest possible words. Writers should keep in mind the reader's knowledge of the subject and their time constraints. So our message should be complete without being wordy. In fact our message should be comprehensive in all respects.

Clarity implies that Communicators have definite purpose of writing and make sure it is clearly communicated.

Clarity demands that each and every point and aspect of our message should be clear to the receiver. In fact message communicated should be unambiguous.

Creativeness means to use different formats to communicate our message. It should include question answer format, graphics etc. Our message should include different formats so that reader may understand our ideas without getting trouble.

Courtesy implies that we should show our expression of respect to the receiver. Courteous message strengthens present relations and makes new friends. Courteous message always makes a place in heart because it shows lot of respect and sincerity . Courtesy is more important and advantageous in business writing than it is in face to face communication and conversations.

Consideration means the message with the receiver in mind. Keep your readers in mind as you write. And try to show reader benefit and interest in reader. In fact we should try to visualise in our readers their desires, problems, emotions, circumstances and possible reaction to our request.

Another school of thought view the seven C's of communication as :

- Credibility
- Context
- Content
- Clarity
- Continuity and Consistency
- Channels; and
- Capability of audiences.

On the above parameters for a successful communication, credibility implies the belief of the communicatee on the communicator regarding the reliability or authenticity of the message or information .While context means the information passed should be context oriented. The content implies the information richness in the form of ideas and facts in the information transmitted. In the case of clarity the message or information passed should be clear and free from ambiguous statements, redundancy etc .While Continuity and consistency imply the flow and organisation of information and consistent usage of terminology etc. The channel implies the appropriate media selected on the basis of the type of the recipients by the communicator. The capability of the audience implies the level of the recipients' in understanding the message or information passed by the communicator.

### 1.5. Levels of Communication

Human communication takes place at various levels. They are :

- extra personal
- Intrapersonal
- interpersonal
- Organisational
- Mass communication.

Communication between human beings and non-human entities is extra personal . Intrapersonal communication takes place within the individual. The brain, an electrochemical system is linked to all parts of the body. The brain provides instructions to all parts of the human body. The interpersonal communication implies communication between person to person or group of persons. Organisational communication takes place at different hierarchical levels which is extremely necessary for the sustenance of any organisation. While mass media communication requires intermediaries such as news paper, television, radio television etc as media for communication.

### 1.6. Flow of Communication

Information flows in an organisation both formally and informally. They are :

- Downward communication
- Upward communication
- Lateral or Horizontal Communication
- Diagonal or Cross-Wise Communication

The downward communication flows from a manager/ director, down the chain of command, while in upward communication when subordinates send reports to inform their superiors or to present their findings and recommendations, the communication flows upward. Lateral or horizontal communication takes place among peer groups or hierarchically equivalent employees. Such communication is often necessary to facilitate coordination, save time, and bridge the communication gap among various departments. Diagonal or cross-wise communication of information flows in all directions and cuts across functions and levels in an organisation.

## 1.7. Barriers of Communication.

The term communication barrier is that which distorts the message . A barrier acts like a sieve, allowing only a part of the message to filter through; as a result, the desired response is not achieved. To communicate effectively and efficiently in an organisation, irrespective of your position, you need to know how the barriers operate and how it can be overcome. The barriers of communication can be broadly divided into the following categories.

- Intrapersonal barriers
- Interpersonal barriers
- Organisational barriers.

### *Intrapersonal Barriers*

Intrapersonal barriers stem from an individual's attitude and habits. Individuals are unique because of their idiosyncrasies. This is mainly because of differences in experience, education, value and personality. Certain common causes which lead to intrapersonal communication barriers are :

**(i) Wrong assumptions :** Many barriers stem from wrong assumptions. Wrong assumptions are generally made because the sender or the receiver does not have adequate knowledge about each other's background or entertains certain false notions, which are fixed in their mind.

**(ii) Varied perceptions :** Individuals in an organisation perceive situations in different ways. Let us take the case of an altercation between two individuals. If you are close to one of them, you are biased. You may perceive your friend's arguments as correct. It is all a matter of varied perception

**(iii) Differing background :** The background of a person plays an important role in how he interpret the message. At times, a person will find it difficult to interpret or appreciate something not experienced by him earlier.

**(iv) Wrong inferences :** Inferences are more dramatic than facts. Inferences supported by facts are essential for professionals when they analyse materials, solve problems and plan procedures. But wrong inferences evolved by individuals lead to barriers to intrapersonal communication .

**(v) Impervious categories :** In general people react positively to information only if it is in consonance with their own views and attitudes. On the other hand, when people receive information that does not conform to their personal views, habits and attitudes, or appears unfavourable to them, they tend to react negatively or even disbelieve. This category of people falls into impervious categories, because they may not be able to accept any deviation from their points of view.

**(vi) Categorical thinking :** People who believe that they 'know it all' are called pansophists. This type of thinking exists in people who feel that they know every thing about a particular subject, and therefore refuse to accept any further information on that topic. This type of thinking can pose a major barrier, leading to a failure in communication.

*Interpersonal Barriers.*

Interpersonal barriers occur due to the inappropriate transactions of words between two or more people. The most important reasons for interpersonal communication barriers are:

**Limited vocabulary** : An inadequate vocabulary of persons can be a major barrier in interpersonal communication. During a speech, if a speaker finds himself at a loss for words, the communication will be very ineffective and will leave a poor impression on the audience.

**Incongruity of verbal and non-verbal messages** : Misinterpreted verbal and nonverbal communications act as another barrier to effective communication. In order to overcome this barrier, non-verbal cues should consistently match verbal messages.

**Emotional outbursts** : In most cases, a moderate level of emotional involvement intensifies communication, making it more personal. But excessive emotional involvement can be a barrier in communication. Extreme anger can create such an emotionally charged environment that rational discussion is just not possible. .Positive emotions like happiness and excitement also interfere in communication, but to a lesser extent than negative feelings

**Communication selectivity** : In a communication process a receiver may sometimes give attention only to part of a message imposing a barrier known as communication selectivity. The receiver does this because he is interested only in that part of the message which may be of use to him. While reading a book, if a reader skips some of the lines or pages in the book then it may cause barrier of communication selectivity.

**Cultural variations** : This is one of the predominant factors in communication failure. In the context of globalisation the cultural variations and use of different languages have immensely influenced all spheres of human activities.

**Poor listening skills** : Poor listening habit is a common obstacle to interpersonal communication. Misunderstanding and conflicts can be mitigated if people listen to the message with due attention. The various distractions that hinder listening can be emotional disturbances, indifference, aggressiveness and wandering attention.

**Noise in the channel** : Noise denotes greatly in the transmission of signals . Noise is any unwanted signal which acts as a hindrance in the flow of communication. It is not necessarily limited to cacophony, but can also occur in visual, audio-visual, written, physical or psychological forms. All these forms of noise communicate extraneous matter which may ally receiver's interest in the message.

### *Organisational Barriers*

In organisations with many levels of communication, messages have a greater chance of being distorted . The main organisational barriers of communication are:

**Too many links of communication chain** : If more links (persons)are involved in communication process, the greater will be the rate of distortion of message or information. Whatever be the reasons for filtering or distorting the message, having too many stations are always detrimental to effective communication in an organisational set up.

**Fear of superiors** : In an organisation, fear of the superiors prevents subordinates from speaking frankly. An employee may not be pleased with the way his boss works but is unable to put his point across because of losing his boss's goodwill. An open environment is conducive to increasing the confidence and goodwill of a communicator.

**Negative tendencies** : Many organisations create working groups . While , some groups are formed according to the demands of the task such as accomplishing a particular project, other small groups such as recreational, social, cultural, seminar etc These groups consist of persons who share similar values, attitudes, opinions, beliefs etc. Nevertheless, on certain situations, it is possible to have communication barrier due to conflict of ideas between members of the group.

**Use of inappropriate media** : A number of media are available for transmission of information. All media may not be suitable for all types of communication. For a successful communication choice of appropriate media for a specific target audience is necessary. Use of inappropriate media will be a hindrance to organisational communication.

**Information overload** : Too much information or data is another hindrance confronted by the receivers for effective communication. Too much information beyond the limit due to information explosion is known as information overload. The usual results of information overload may lead to disinterest among users. Very often vital information may be mixed up with irrelevant information in the information flood which may be ignored by the receiver .

## 1.8. Forms of communication

The major types or forms of communication can be categorised as :

- Verbal communication ;and
- Non-verbal communication

### *1.8.1. Verbal communication*

The basis of communication is the interaction between people. Verbal communication is one way for people to communicate face-to –face, Some of the major components of verbal communication are sound, words, speaking and language. Verbal communication can be categorised into the following types or modes of communication.

- Oral Communication
- Audio-visual communication
- Electronic communication
- Written Communication

*Oral Communication*

Oral communication is a method of communication through speech. The oral forms of communication include face-to-face conversations, telephone conversations, meetings, seminars, conferences, dictation, instructions, presentations, group discussions, interview, video conferences, voice conferences etc.

Oral communication is characteristic of its immediacy and personal touch which may be difficult to capture in other forms of communication. This is because, the physical senses like vision, hearing and touch can be used by the speaker as well as the listener.

Oral communication can be divided into two types viz direct and indirect oral communication. If an individual speaks to another person or a group of persons, face to face or through any media is direct oral communication. While when a message or information is transmitted through a person other than the originator of the message it is called indirect oral communication.

The essential factors for a successful oral communication are well modulated voice, quality, pitch, volume and rate of words. Voice is an integral part of our physical , mental and emotional make up. It is an important factor in shaping our relationships with others. A person's voice is very often regarded as an indicator of his character. Quality is a characteristic that distinguishes one voice from another, though both may have the same degree of pitch, rate and volume. The pitch, the highness and lowness of the speaker's voice is another factor in successful oral communication. The volume can be achieved by an efficient use of the breath and the resonating chambers. Other factors which need to be borne in mind for attaining proper volume are the size and acoustics of the room, the number of listeners and the level of background noise. Rate refers to the speed at which a person speaks. It is determined by four interrelated factors : the duration of sounds, the number of words spoken per minute, the duration and frequency of pauses.

The overall tempo of speech is also affected by the mood

appropriate to the occasion. For example, a heightened rate of speech helps to create moods of joy, fear, anger and surprise. To express sorrow, or disgust a slow delivery of words is better. On an average, a rate between 130 and 170 words per minute is advisable in a normal situation.

### *Audio- Visual Communication*

The term audio-visual may refer to works with both a sound and a visual component, the production or use of such works or to equipment used to create and present such works. Computer presentation, slide tape presentation, films and television programme are examples of audio-visual presentation. In a typical presentation, the presenter provides the audio by speaking and supplements it with a series of images projected onto a screen, either from a slide projector, or from a computer connected to a LCD projector using a presentation programme. The strength of audio-visual communication is its ability to heave massive amounts of information at us. Audio-visual media is a high volume media because it sends so many messages at one time. It supports the phrase 'a picture is worth a thousand words' because audio-visual media delivers millions of messages to those who consume it.

### *Electronic Communication*

Electronic communication comes in many forms, and indeed one of the most common and well known is email, Email was created as a way of contacting an individual around the same time that the Internet was created.

Electronic communication also comes in the form of text messaging. Text messaging is a form of electronic communication that is similar to email, but instead requires you to use mobile phone and a carrier. The carrier will be able to send your message over telephone network, whilst the phone will be used to write the text in the first place.

### *Written Communication*

Written communication is another form of communication for transmitting and receiving information. It has great significance in the contemporary society. It is an innovative activity of the mind. Speech came before writing. But writing is more unique and formal than speech. Effective writing involves careful choice of words, their organisation in correct order in sentences formation as well as cohesive composition of sentences. Also writing is more valid and reliable than speech. Some of the characteristics of written communication are that it:

- has a more formal perspective, suggesting greater authority and trustworthiness;
- can be a potential record, capable of extended life and being used again and again;
- can be extracted in parts or portions and can be authentically quoted;
- is suitable for reading at an individual's on best reading time, speed and place; and
- is accessible to a large readership which can also lead to the benefit of expert criticism and review by peers.

The written communication has a number of advantages over other modes of communication. The major advantages are :

(i) Written communication helps in laying down apparent principles, policies and rules for running of an organisation;

(ii) It is a permanent means of communication;

(iii) It assists in proper delegation of responsibilities. While, in case of oral communication it is impossible to fix and delegate responsibilities on the ground of speech as it can be taken back by the speaker or he may refuse to acknowledge;

(iv) Written communication is more precise and explicit;

(v) Effective written communication develops and enhances an organisation's image; It provides ready records and references.

(vi) Legal defences can depend upon written communication as it provides valid records.

Of course, the written communication has certain disadvantages too. The disadvantages are:

(a) Written communication does not save upon the costs. It costs huge in terms of stationery and the manpower employed in writing;

(b) Also, if the receivers of the written message are separated by distance and if they need to clear their doubts, the response is not spontaneous;

(c) Written communication is time consuming as the feed back is not immediate. The encoding and sending of message takes time;

(d) Effective written communication requires great skills and competencies in language and vocabulary use. Poor writing skills and quality have negative impact on organisation's reputation;

(e) Too much paper work and e-mail burden are involved.

***Types of Written Communication.***

The written communication can be categorised into two forms of communication. They are :

- Creative writing; and
- Technical writing.

**Creative Writing :** Creative writing involves a certain amount of creativity in individual. In addition to a good command of language a creative writer should have flair for writing. A creative writer, applying his/her rhetoric abilities of using a language, effectively portrays a vivid picture of an event or activity in an imaginative style with a deep perception of the environment in which the event or activity takes place and the characters involved in it. Writings such as novel, short story, poetry, drama etc can be considered as products of creative writing.

**Technical Writing :** Technical writing unlike creative

writing, is not a reality but rather the recreation of what was once a reality, namely narrating a given job, to meet a social, economic, commercial or techno-economic need. Technical writing differs from other types of writing in many ways .But the predominant characteristics that distinguish technical writing from other expository writing is the reporting of technical data, which necessarily include tabular presentation of data, illustrations etc.

Technical articles, research reports, patents, house journals, trade literature, manuals, etc are examples to the products of technical writing.

**Channels of Communication** : The channels through which the oral or written communication transmitted include formal viz Downward, upward, horizontal and lateral; and Informal such as Grapevine, exchange of information at casual private or public meetings etc.

While formal channel is that which is planned, organised and systematic, informal channel include all the unorganised, unplanned and non-systematic. Formal media include print media and are generally graphic though there are a few kinds which are oral . Some are a combination of these. Examples: Lectures, conferences, public addresses, class room teaching, demonstrations etc. On the other hand informal media generally is an oral form of communication and includes tea-talks, travel talks, information exchanges at casual meetings. 'Invisible college' and 'Technological Gatekeepers are two most important examples of informal communication media.

### *1.8.2. Non-verbal communication*

Non-verbal communication is usually understood as the process of communication through sending and receiving wordless mostly visual messages. Messages can be communicated through gestures and touch (Hapatic communication), by body language or posture, by facial expression and eye contact . Meaning can also be communicated through object or artefacts such as clothing, hairstyles, symbols and icons. Much of the study of nonverbal communication has focused on face-to face interaction, where it can be classified into three principal areas: environmental conditions where communication takes place, the physical characteristics of the communicators and behaviours of communicators during interaction.

The first scientific study of nonverbal communication was Charles Darwin's book, 'The Expression of the Emotions in Man and Animals'. He argued that all mammals show emotion reliably in their faces. Studies now range across a number of fields including linguistics, semiotics and social psychology.

The following are some of the significant characteristics of nonverbal communication.

- Nonverbal messages primarily communicate emotions, attitudes
- Nonverbal cues substitute for, contradict, emphasise or regulate verbal message
- Nonverbal cues are often ambiguous
- Nonverbal cues are continuous
- Nonverbal cues are more reliable
- Nonverbal cues are culture bound
- Nonverbal behaviour always has communicative value
- Nonverbal communication is powerful

**Clothing and Bodily Characteristics** : Elements such as physique, height, weight, hair , skin colour, gender , odours and clothing send nonverbal messages during interaction. Research into height has generally found that taller people are perceived as being more impressive. Often people try to make themselves taller, for example, standing on a platform, when they want to make more of an impact with their speaking.

**Physical Environment** : Environmental factors such as furniture, architectural style, interior decoration, lighting conditions, colours, temperature, noise and music affect the behaviour of communicators during interaction.

**Proxemics :** Proxemics is the study of how people use and perceive the physical space around them. The space between the sender and the receiver of a message influences the way the message is interpreted, The perception and use of space varies significantly across cultures and different settings within cultures, Space in nonverbal communication may be divided into four main categories: intimate, social, personal and public space.

**Chronemics :** Chronemics is the study of use of time in nonverbal communication. The way we perceive time, structure our time and react to time are powerful communication tools, and help set the stage for communication. Time perception includes punctuality and willingness to wait, the speed of speech and how long people are willing to listen . The timing and frequency of an action as well as the tempo and rhythm of communications within an interaction contributes to the interpretation of nonverbal messages.

### *Movement and Body Positions*

**Kinesics :** Kinesics is the study of body language, how people communicate through posture, gesture, stance and movement. Posture can be used to determine a participant's degree of attention or involvement, the difference in status between communicators and the level of fondness a person has for the other communicator.

A gesture is a nonverbal bodily movement intended to express meaning. They may be articulated with the hands, arms or body, and also include movements of the head, face and eyes, such as winking, nodding, or rolling one's eyes. The boundary between language and gesture, or verbal and nonverbal communication, can be hard to identify. Gestures can be categorised as either speech –independent or speech related. In an oral communication speakers use hands for making various types of gestures like enumerative, descriptive, locative, symbolic and emphatic so as to make the speech more effective.

**Eye Contact :** Of the five sense organs, the eyes are the most expressive. They act as the window of the mind, and can express elemental passions as well as varying moods of person. The study of the role of eyes in nonverbal communication is sometimes referred as 'oculesics'. Eye contact can indicate interest, attention and involvement. Studies have pointed out that people use their eyes to indicate their interest and with more than the frequently recognised actions of winking and slight movement of the eyebrows. Eye contact and facial expressions provide important social and emotional information

**Haptics :** Haptics is the study of touching as nonverbal communication. This includes handshakes, holding hands, kissing, back slapping, pat on the shoulder and brushing an arm. The meaning conveyed from touch is highly dependent upon the context of the situation, the relationship between communicators and the manner of touch.

## 1.9. Conclusion

Technical communication plays an important role in an organisation, whether it is business enterprise, an industry or an academic institution . All managerial or administrative activities involve communication, be it planning, organising, recruiting, coordinating, or decision making. Communication serves as an instrument to measure the success or growth of an organisation.

## REFERENCES

Garvey, WD(1979): Communication: the essence of science facilitating information exchange among libraries, scientists, engineers and students.Oxford, Pergamon Press.

Feather, John and Sturges, Paul (1997): International Encyclopedia of Information and Library Science.London, Routledge.

McQuail, D and Windahl, S(1993) Comunication models. London , Longman

Meenakshi Raman and Sangeeta Sharma(2004) Technical communication:Principless and practice.New York, Oxford University Press.

Shannon, C and Weaver, W (1949): The mathematical theory of communication. Illinois, University of Illinois Press.

Tubbs, SL and Moss, S(2000) Human communication, New York, McGraw Hill.

Wikipedia, the free encyclopedia.wikipedia.org/wiki

# 2
# Technical Communication

## 2.1. INTRODUCTION

Technical communication is a method of researching and creating information about technical processes or products directed to an audience through media. The information must be relevant to the intended audience. Technical communicators often work collaboratively to create deliverable products for various media including paper, video and internet.. The deliverable products include online help, user manuals, technical manuals, white papers, specifications, Process and procedure manuals, industrial videos, data sheets, journal articles, patents, training business papers, technical reports etc. Technical domains can be of any kind, including soft and hard sciences, high technology including computers and software, consumer electronics, and business processes and practices.

The origin of technical communication has been variously attributed to Ancient Greece, the renaissance and the middle of 20$^{th}$ century. However, a clear trend towards the professional field can be seen from the First world war on, growing out of the need for technology–based documentation in the military, manufacturing, electronic and aerospace industries. In the United States, two organisations concerned with improving the practice of technical communication were founded on the East Coast in 1953. They were the Society of Technical Writers and the Association of Technical Writers and Editors. These organisations merged in 1957 to form the Society of Technical Writers and Editors, a predecessor of the current Society for Technical Communication(STC). In the United Kingdom, the Institute of Scientific and Technical Communicators(ISTC) was formed in 1972 by the amalgamation of three existing associations : the presentation of Technical Information Group(established in 1948), the Technical Publications Association(established in 1953) and the Institute of Technical Publicity and publications (established in 1963).

## 2.2. WHAT IS TECHNICAL COMMUNICATION?

Technical communications are created and distributed by most employees in service organisations today, especially by professional staff and management. Writing well is difficult and time consuming, and writing in a technical way and about technical subjects compounds the difficulties. The entire point of communications is to disseminate useful information. To be useful, information must be understood and acted upon. Fortunately, tools and techniques are available to make writing more accessible and easy to understand.

Effective communications require quality content, language, format, and more. The entire point of communications is to disseminate information; this is where written content comes in. To present the appropriate content, it is imperative to understand one's audience and writing purpose. If a document does not communicate the information that the writer intends and what he or she wants the reader to understand, then the communication is meaningless.

The various designations of those who are engaged in the technical communication include:

- Technical writer
- Technical editor

- Information Architect
- Usability expert
- User interface designer
- Technical artist
- Technical trainer
- Technical translator etc

## 2.3. TECHNICAL WRITING

Technical writing is a form of technical communication.

It is the presentation of information that helps the reader to solve a particular problem. Technical writers write, design, and /or edit proposals, manuals, web pages, lab reports, news letters and many other kinds of professional documents. Wikipedia defines Technical writing, a form of technical communication is a style of writing used in fields as diverse as computer hardware and software, engineering, chemistry, the aerospace industry, robotics, finance, consumer electronics, and biotechnology. Technical writers explain technology and related ideas to technical and non technical audiences. This could mean, for example, telling a programmer how to use a library software or telling a consumer how to operate a television remote control.

Pauley and Riordan views technical writing is difficult to define, and researchers in the field have not agreed on a definition. Technical writing is the practical writing that people do as part of their jobs, whatever their position – from executive to middle manager, from specialised research scientist to secretary - people generate documents as part of their responsibilities.

## 2.4. OBJECTIVES OF TECHNICAL WRITING

The major objectives of technical writing are : to inform, to instruct; and to persuade target audience. The purpose of most of the technical writing is to inform people matters relating to their work environment, developments in a field of study, introduction of an equipment to the customers etc. While intention of certain technical writing is to instruct the target audience in the procedures followed in the working of an instrument, instruction in the form to execute a specific work etc. But the purpose of certain technical writings is in the category of persuading readers for a specific course of action. Writings of an author may persuade a reader to resolve a particular problem that he met with. The technical writers may focus on one or more objectives in a technical writing.

## 2.5. WRITING SITUATIONS

The writing situations can be primarily categorised into two groups.

- Individual Writing; and
- Corporate writing

### Individual Writing

Individual writing is carried out by individual efforts, motivated by an urge to communicate on a subject of public interest or a compelling situation in the case of a research scholar. The writings may be related to scientific, socio-economic, political or in the cultural spheres. These writings may be in the form of popular articles, letters to the editor, technical articles, etc. Most of these types of writings are undertaken by individuals who have necessary subject expertise, experience and competency.

### Corporate Writing

Corporate or organisational writings are generated by persons or group of persons as part of fulfilling the objectives and functions of the parent organisations. Educational institutions, R & D institutions, Learned societies or associations, governmental organisations, mass communication institutions and other types of offices generate various types of technical writings.

The writing situations exist in educational institutions may be in the form of preparation of course materials, work book, text books, reference guides, self instruction manuals, articles, research studies etc. The writing situation in R & D institutions the researchers focussed their writings in the specialised areas of research and development of the parent organisation. These may be brought in the form of working papers, technical reports, house journal etc. While in the case of associations or learned bodies, the writing situation will be to inform the members of the association, the developments in the domain through the generation of journals, research reports, news letters etc.

The governmental bodies such as legislature, executive and judiciary are considered the biggest generators and users of information in a country. A lot of technical writings are brought out by the governmental bodies in the form of bills, Acts, ordinances, administration reports, commission reports, financial reports, policy reports, legal and regulatory documents etc. The institutions engaged in mass communication generate technical writings in the form of news analysis reports, comments and reviews, feature articles, news digests etc.

The writing situation which may arise in offices as part of administrative procedures generates quite a good number of technical writings in the form of letters and correspondence, personal evaluation reports, office memoranda, administration reports, financial reports, agenda and minutes of statutory committee meetings, briefing documents, house journals, news letters, discussion papers, circulars, profiles of individuals, statement of internal plans and policy documents etc.

## 2.6. FORMS OF TECHNICAL WRITING

The following are the various forms or categories of technical writings. Of course, this may not be an exhaustive categorisation due to certain cross Classification.

- Letters & correspondences
- Popular articles
- Technical articles
- Memoranda

- Bills, Acts, Ordinances
- Administration Report
- Financial Reports
- Patents
- Standards & Specifications
- Dissertation/Theses
- Project proposals
- Project Reports
- Research Monograph
- Commission Reports
- Minutes
- Course Materials
- Manuals
- Trade Literature
- Technical Reports
- Abstracts
- Review Articles
- Information Digest
- State of the Art Reports
- Trend Reports
- Guides to Literature etc
- Web sites, Blog and other forms of digital contents creation

Broadly speaking, technical writing can be categorised into three types, depending on the style of writing, the level of knowledge transferred and the target audience.

**End User Assistance:** These information products help a user to understand how to use a technical software or hardware product. User manuals for computer software, hardware, household products, medical equipments, cell phones, smart phones and other consumer items belong to this category.

**Traditional technical documentation:** Here the objective of the writer is to communicate with a specific audience. Maintenance guides, application repair manuals, engineering specifications, research papers, research reports, works of reference, annual reports, technical articles belong to this category.

**Marketing communication:** Product catalogues, brochures, advertisements, contents of web sites, press releases etc

Technical writing is often associated with online help and user manuals. However, technical writers create many other forms of technical content. These include product release notes, product troubleshooting guides, product user guides, tutorials, software installation guides, API programmers' guides, legal disclaimers, policies and procedures, business proposals, white paper etc.

## 2,7. CHARACTERISTICS OF TECHNICAL WRITING

According to Cunningham and Hartley the major characteristics of technical writing are:

### (i) Specific Audience

It is essential that the technical writer understands the reader's background and needs. Making the documentation too technical can confuse the reader. The document is meaningless if the intended audience does not understand what the writer wants to communicate. Writers who are well aware of their audiences are in a position to give a solution to their problems. In fact the specific subject or topic selected for each form of technical writing is focused towards specific audience. A course material on a specific subject is generated for the students as the specific audience whereas in the case of a commission report the specific audience is the higher authorities like the government. In the case of trade literature on a specific product the consumer is the specific audience while general public is the specific audience for a popular article.

### (ii) Objective Language

The objective language that is in tune with the audience

level or standard is used in the technical writing. The objectives of technical communication are to inform, to instruct or to persuade the reader population. Hence the tone of the language used should be oriented towards the objective/s. The technical writing demands simplicity of language and clarity of expression. It should be clear and concise so that the text becomes easier to grasp and understand. In fact present the contents in a language that is easily understandable and reader-oriented.

### (iii) Presentational organisation

Hartley views technical writing as presentational. Presentational writing employs devices that enable readers to assimilate information at a glance. Technical writing has a very obvious composition that makes it easy for the reader to follow along. Solid structure is needed with technical writing as it allows the audience to easily access the information as needed. Structural organisation, specific format, style of presentations are the significant characteristics of technical writing.

### (iv) Visual aids

Non-textual or visual aid is another significant characteristics of technical writing. Visual aids such as tables, graphs, bar diagrams, pie diagrams, charts, figures etc are extensively used in technical writing. In fact, technical writing presents the writing supported by well designed illustrations and photographs wherever necessary to draw the attention of the target group.

## 2.8. PRINCIPLES OF TECHNICAL WRITING

Saracevic and Wood point out that the technical writing to be effective, it has to adhere to principles of good writing in general and offer more specific principles given below.

**Accuracy** : make sure that the material selected for technical writing is accurate to the most up-to-date information available.

**Logical progression**: follow a logical progression of thought.

**Simplicity:** keep it simple.

**Word choice:** Select words for precise communication, use jargon with discretion.

**Analogy:** make liberal use of examples familiar to the sensitivities of the audience.

**Sensitivity:** follow any restrictions and adhere to the sensitivities of the audience.

- Supported by illustrations and examples; and
- Physical production

## 2.9. EFFECTIVENESS OF TECHNICAL WRITING

The following are some of the parameters that can be used to measure effectiveness of technical writings.

- Writers must have unambiguous understanding of readers whom the writing is meant for and the purpose of writing;
- An abiding interest in reading, general as well as specialised material, relevant to the areas of work of the writer ;
- Quality of contents in terms of authenticity, reliability, authority adequacy, currency etc.;
- Structural organisation of contents in terms of logical arrangement of themes and sub-themes of contents, dividing them into sections and subsections with main and sub-headings;
- Putting the organised contents into a language which presents the ideas with clarity and lucidity, resulting final draft of manuscript in terms of readability, positioning of illustrations appropriately to go with the textual matter and related aspects.

## 2.10. TECHNICAL WRITING PROCESS

The goal of technical writing process is to generate an effective technical document for the specific target audience. To accomplish this, an experienced writer goes through three distinct phases of activities such as :

- Prewriting
- Writing
- Postwriting

**Prewriting**

Prewriting connotes the planning of the proposed form of technical writing.

Planning is a key activity in writing any technical document. Better writing results from better planning. To plan effectively the writer should consider the following aspects.

**(i) Consider the audience, goal and constraints :** The writer should consider, Who is my audience? Who will read this document? What are the beliefs of the audience about the topic? What form do they expect the document to have?. In respect of the goal of the document the basic message and purpose of the document may be considered. The writer should also consider what are the physical and social constraints which affect both ability of the writer to generate the document and reader' ability to respond to it.

**(ii) Find the gist of the document :** Here the writer can plan the basic facts to be included in the document, determine what are the sources to be consulted, determine the strategy to be applied for generating the document, plan an outline of the document and determine the tone of the message to be communicated to the audience.

**(iii) Develop Specifications :** In this stage consider what should be the format in which the proposed document is to be generated and what are the various types of visual aids to be included in the proposed document to be generated.

**(iv) Develop a Production Schedule :** Developing a production schedule is an important task in this stage. A production schedule is a chronological list of the activities required to generate the document. Time schedule for various activities are to be included such as, preparation of preliminary draft, editing and revising of draft, preparation of final draft, production of final report etc. All these time schedules for various activities depend up on the number of person/s to be involved in the generation of the document.

### Writing Stage

In the writing stage the writer produces the draft. In this stage the planning that you have made in the prewriting stage is materialising in this verbal plane. You try to put on paper the words that explain the ideas in the outline. Theoretically, if you have planned thoroughly and arrived at a clear sense of the gist, all you need to do is flesh out the outline and describe the visual aids. The object of drafting is to generate writing and to improve it until it effectively conveys your message to the reader. Clarifying and discovering are the two important facets of drafting. As you draft, you clarify your ideas for your reader and yourself. But by writing it is also discovery and in this sense the preliminary drafting stage complements planning. As you draft, you may immediately conceive nascent ideas or new ways to present an example.

### Drafting Strategies

Experts have suggested a number of drafting strategies or course of action in the drafting process. They are:

- Prototyping
- Iterative development; and
- Spiral development

In the prototyping strategy construction of a prototype or miniature form of the proposed document contains all key points under each heading and subheadings. There are three types of prototyping possible viz rapid prototyping; model prototyping and throwaway prototyping. In the rapid prototyping the basic ideas are written quickly as possible by the writer while in model prototyping or basing the draft on the basis of a model are to be followed by a writer in a previously published document. In the case of a throwaway prototyping or developing a document it will act as a test to see whether the document conveys the message effectively.

The iterative development strategy of drafting entails composing a draft and then making multiple revision of it, each time focusing on only one element. While spiral development means developing the most difficult section of the document first and then analysing and revising it. The less difficult portions of the document are drafted later.

### Guidelines for Effective Drafting

For an effective, efficient and easier drafting the writer should sense a number of aspects. Huckin has suggested the following guidelines for effective drafting.

(i) State your purpose explicitly. Researchers have found that most readers want a broad, general statement that helps them comprehend the details.

(ii) Make the topic of each section and paragraph clear. Use head. Put topic sentences at the beginning of paragraphs.

(iii) Use the same terminology throughout. Do not confuse the reader by changing names.

(iv) For an audience with little prior knowledge about a topic, use the familiar to explain the unfamiliar. Provide examples, operational definitions, analogies, and illustrations. These devices invite your reader to become imaginatively involved with the topic and make it interesting.

(v) For readers familiar with a topic, do not belabour the basics. Use accepted terminology.

(vi) If you want your readers remember main ideas, structure your document hierarchically ; if you want them to remember details, use a list of format.

(vii) Write clear sentences. You should try to write short sentences (under 25 words), to rely on the active voice, to employ parallelism, and to use words the reader understands. You will not always achieve these goals in the first draft, but you will be amazed how much you can achieve, even in first draft, if you develop an awareness of them.

(viii) Make your writing interesting. You create interest by using devices that help readers 'picture' the topic, thus imaginatively involving them in it. The picturing devices apply to both your writing and your visual aids. When writing, include helpful comparisons, common examples, brief sceneries and narratives. Visual devices include any graphics that help the reader visualise the topic from photographs and drawings to tables and graphs.

## Post Writing Stage

Post writing stage entails revising and editing of the draft document until it conveys the message effectively. You must evaluate every element such as word choice, sentences, paragraphs, overall organisation and effectiveness of the message. Schriver observes that revision is a three step process: you detect, diagnose, and solve problems with your draft. Spelling, sentence structure, grammar, paragraph structure, the overall organisation and the strategy used in the document to convey the message etc should be examined thoroughly in the revising of the technical document. If the draft is prepared in computer by using a word processor most of the problems enlisted above can be rectified very effectively and efficiently.

The finishing stage of the document consists of two activities such as editing and producing the final document. The editing means making a consistent and accurate text. Check the proper use of punctuation, format of the page, style, accuracy of the facts etc.

The Production of the final document has two dimensions: the physical completion of the document and its psychological completion. Physical completion means typing or printing the final document whereas psychological completion means attending to your emotions as you near completion and managing your time schedule properly.

## 2.10. HOW TO EVALUATE A TECHNICAL DOCUMENT?

A finished document can be evaluated to assess the validity of the document. The following checklist or criteria can be used to evaluate a technical document.

- Objectivity of the technical document
- Accuracy and Authenticity
- Organisation of the document
- Clarity of Presentation
- Documentation
- Brevity
- Consistency and Precision
- Language
- Physical production

## 2.11. TECHNICAL WRITING SKILLS VS INFORMATION PROFESSIONALS

Information professionals met with a number of writing situations call for writing skills for the generation of quality documents. This is because the expanding library and information systems, services and management call for writing skills of the highest quality. The writing situations of information professionals can be viewed under three perspectives. They are : i) Individual development, ii) Organisational Requirements and' iii) Professional services.

Technical writing skills will enable the information professionals in his individual development in the career. The writing skills can be achieved by the professionals from the library schools themselves through the technical writing practices such as preparation of assignments, projects, dissertations and thesis etc. This will help the professionals to get more and more chances in the career as a good communicator and help in an all pervasive development of an individual.

Libraries and Information centres demand a number of writing situations as part of the scientific management. A number of documents in the form of office communication such as memo, memoranda, personal evaluation files, proposals, reports etc have to be prepared by the information managers as part of administration. In such situation an information manager with good writing skills will excel as a good administrator in the organisation.

Librarians and Information managers can generate quite a good number of value added information services and products. In the present day information environment such services are warranted and highly appreciated by the user community. In the information condensation and repackaging and presentation of the products and services in the form of abstracts, information digest, review article, status report, trend report etc. information professionals should require technical writing skills. Technical writing skills of information professionals are helpful to render quality information services to users on demand or in anticipation

## REFERENCES


Booth, PF(1991) Report writing, Huntington, Kings Ripton

Chandler, H E (1983) Technical writer's handbook. Ohio, American Society for Metals.

Eisenberg, A (1989) Writing well for technical profession. New York, Harper & Row

Gerson, SJ and Gerson SM ( 1992) Technical writing: Process and products

Hartley, Peter (1991) Writing for industry. The Technical writing Teacher. 18(2) :162-69.

Huckin, Thomas(1983) A cognitve approach to readability. In New essays in technical and scientific communication research ed by Paul V Anderson, et al. New York, Baywood.

Killingsworth,M J and Gilbertson, M(1988) How can text and graphics be integrated effectively. In solving problems in technical writing. Ed.by Beene and White. New York, Oxford.

Meenakshi Raman and Sangeetha Sharma(2004) Technical communication: Principless and practice, London, Oxford University Press.

Mills, GS and Walier, JA(1986): Technical writing. 5th edn. New York, Hold Rinehart.

Pauley, Steven E and Riordan, Daniel G(1996) Technical report writing today. Delhi, AITBS.

Reep, DC (1991) Technical writing, principles, strategies and readings. Boston, Allyn and Bacon.;Cliffs, Prentice Hall.

# 3

# Language Used as the Medium of Communication

## 3.1. INTRODUCTION

Language may refer either to the specifically human capacity for acquiring and using complex systems of communication, or to a specific instance of such a system to complex communication. About 3000-6000 languages that are spoken by humans today are the most salient examples, but natural languages can also be based on visual rather than auditory stimuli, for example in sign languages and written language. Codes and other kinds of artificially constructed communication systems such as those used for computer programming can also be called languages. A language in this sense is a system of signs for encoding and decoding information.

The human language faculty is thought to be fundamentally different from and of much higher complexity than those of other species. Human language is highly complex in that it is based on a set of rules relating to symbols to their meanings, thereby forming an infinite number of possible innovative utterances from a finite number of elements. Humans acquire language through social interaction. The use of language has become deeply entrenched in human culture and, apart from being used to communicate and share information.

Language is an effective medium or tool of communication. It implies language as a system of communication that enables humans to cooperate. This stresses the social functions of language and the fact that humans use it to express themselves and to manipulate objects in their environment. This view of language is associated with the study of language in a functional or pragmatic framework, as well as in socio-linguistics anthropology.

Human language is unique in comparison to other forms of communication such as those used by animals, because it allows humans to produce an infinite set of utterances from a finite set of elements. The symbols and grammatical rules of any particular language are largely arbitrary, so that the system can only be acquired through social interaction. The known systems of communication used by animals, on the other hand, can only express a finite number of utterances that are mostly genetically transmitted. Human language is also unique when compared to any other kinds of communication system.

Various types of languages such as spoken language, written language, sign language, etc are used to exchange ideas from person to person/s. Spoken and written languages are known as natural languages or human languages. A common progression for natural languages is that they are considered to be first spoken and then written, and then an understanding and explanation of their grammar is attempted. Spoken and sign languages contain a phonological system that governs how sounds or visual symbols are used to form sequences known as words, and a syntactic system that governs how words and morphemes are used to form phrases and utterances. Written languages use visuals symbols to represent the sounds of the spoken languages, but they still require syntactic rules that govern the production of meaning from sequences of words. There are basically two ways in which we communicate with each other-through writing as well as verbally. Of course speech is primary, and is acquired spontaneously in early infancy through exposure. Writing is learned much later. Also the written language cannot be seen in isolation from the spoken language. In general, our understanding of written language depends on our knowledge of the corresponding spoken language and on our linguistic competence in general.

## 3.2. SPOKEN LANGUAGE VS WRITTEN LANGUAGE

There are a number of differences between spoken language and written language. Spoken language is used in face to face interaction and occurs as part of a dialogue. In fact, there is reciprocal exchange in which both reception and production play a part. But, written language is non-reciprocal and non interactive, in that the reader and writer are not visible to each other. Spoken language is composed spontaneously as it is spoken, and is mostly unplanned and relatively unpredictable. While written language is published, planned, edited, drafted before it appears in print. Written language is permanent, as it is published whereas spoken language, which has to be processed in real time, in lock-step with the speaker. The written language reflects, to a large extent, the elements and rules that together constitute the grammar of the language. Written language is more conservative than spoken language, which has to be processed in real time. Spoken language is much less structured than written language. Both spoken and written language show stylistic variation from formal to informal style. Spoken language shows more variation than written language. While written language shows relatively less stylistic variation and more homogeneity, since it is used mostly for formal purposes. Spoken language is context- dependent while written language is decontextualised,i.e it has to stand on its own. Written language depends on its ability to create durable and accurate records for reference in the present and future.

## 3.3. FUNCTIONS OF LANGUAGE

Language, perhaps began because human beings needed a greater degree of cooperation with each other in order to survive, and the cooperation required an effective communication system. It is a well established fact that effective communication is made possible with the help of language. In fact the primary function of a language is to convey information. Language can also be used to communicate feelings and emotions and it is known as phatic communication. Language also has an indirect function in providing information about the communicator in respect of his social background, occupation, region which he represents.

## 3.4. CHARACTERISTICS OF LANGUAGE

The important characteristics of language are the following.

### Use of Sound Signals

Human language is a signalling system which utilises sound signals to express meanings.

### Abstractness

Abstractness is an important feature of language. It is that which makes all generalisation possible. When we talk about a number of similar items, we can group them through abstraction, labelling their common features. This makes it possible to categorise, so that we need not constantly redefine the new information we receive.

### Language is Restricted

When we think and translate our thoughts into language, some meaning is lost in the process. No symbol or word can transmit the exact reality. That is one reason you sometimes find yourself saying that you cannot find words to express your feelings.

### Language is artificial

Language is created by people. It does not exist in isolation or outside the minds of people. It is created by humans as they need it. Every symbol is attached to a particular thought or thing.

### Arbitrariness

There is no direct relationship between a word and the idea

or object it represents. People speaking a particular language accept the fact that certain symbols or sounds will represent a particular thing. For example, there is no relation between the word 'Elephant' and the four legged huge animal.

### Language is Repetitive

Whatever language you use, it has the capacity for redundancy or repetition. This may either imprve or impede effective communication.

### Recursiveness

Recursiveness is the characteristics of language which enables you to generate any number of sentences using the same basic grammatical templates. It also allows you to express any idea, thought, or feeling using the same finite vocabulary. If you use your imagination, you can see that sentence can continue to any length if you keep on adding qualifying clauses for every noun. This is because the recursive quality of language enables you to keep repeating the relative clause pattern.

### Displacement

Human beings can communicate events separated by space and time. For example language can be used to express an event which happened years back, has happened today and will happen tomorrow in London, China or in moon.

### Structure Dependence

Language is not a haphazard list of individual sounds. Most sounds become meaningful only when they are combined with other sounds. This organisation of language into two layers – a layer of sounds, which combines into a layer of larger units such as words is known as duality of structure. A communication system with duality is much more flexible than one without it.

### Creativity

Language is indeed very creative and you can marvel at its

ability to generate so many words every day. In fact, it is essentially a creative process. There is another dimension to the essential creativity of human communication, and this dimension may be called functional creativity. This basically refers to the ability of human beings to evolve more complex communication systems, as the complexity of their life increases. As human beings have progressed from nomadic life to the more stable homestead and agrarian society, industrial society, post industrial society and information society or knowledge society, language has also evolved to meet the demands of each type of society.

## 3.5. LANGUAGE VARIATIONS

In sociolinguistics, variation in language use among speakers or groups of speakers is a principal concern. Such variation may occur in pronunciation, word choice, or even preferences for particular grammatical patterns. Studies in the field of sociolinguistics typically take a sample population and interview them, assessing the realisation of certain sociolinguistics variables. William Labov specifies the ideal sociolinguistic variables to

- be high in frequency
- have a certain immunity from conscious suppression
- be an integral part of larger structure; and
- be easily quantified on a linear scale.

Phonetic variables tend to meet these criteria and are often used, as are grammatical variables and, more rarely, lexical variables.

There are variations in the use of language due to various factors such as age, geography, gender etc.

### Variations associated with Age

There are several different types of age-based variation one may see within a population. They are: vernacular of a subgroup with membership characterised by a specific age range, age –

graded variation, and indications of linguistics change in progress. For example, subgroup vernacular is the speech of street youth. They have their own 'language'. The reasons are : to enhance their own cultural identity; to identify with each other; to exclude others; and to make feelings of fear or admiration from the outside world. Strictly speaking, this is not truly age-based, since it does no apply to all individuals of that age bracket within the community.

Age-graded variation is a stable variation which varies within a population based on age. People tend to use linguistic forms which were prevalent when they reached adulthood. So, in the case of linguistic change in progress, one would expect to see variation over a broader range of ages.

## Variations Associated with Geography

A commonly studied source of variation is regional dialects. Dialectology studies variations in language based primarily on geographic distribution and their associated features. Sociolinguists concerned with grammatical and phonological features that correspond to regional areas are often called dialectologists.

## Variations Associated with Gender

Men and women, on average, tend to use slightly different language styles. These differences tend tc be quantitative rather than qualitative. It is stated that the use of a particular speaking style by women more than men do is akin to saying that men are taller than women. A recent study reported by Deborah Tannen compared gender differences in language as more similar to cultural differences. Comparing conversational goal, she argued that men have a report style, aiming to communicate factual information, whereas women have a rapport style, more concerned with building and maintaining relationships. Such differences are pervasive across media, including in face to face conversation.

## The standard Language

The standard language is that which is used in print, and is normally taught in schools and is learnt by foreigners. It is a variety of language that is codified i.e grammar books, dictionaries are written on the basis of this variety. Moreover, it is used in news broadcasts, and spoken by the educated people. Many people consider this variety as the 'real language' and those that differ from it as dialects. In technical writing, standard language is used as the medium of communication.

## REFERENCES

Fromkin, J(1988) Teach yourself linguistics. Hodder and Stoughton

Lavov, W(1966) The social stratification of English in New york city. Washington, Centre for Applied Linguistics.

Tannen, Deborah(1991)You just don't understand: women and men in conversation. London, Virago.

Taudgill, P (1974) Sociolinguistics: An introduction. Harmondsworth, Penguin

# 4

# Reader, Writer and Readability of Text

## 4.1. INTRODUCTION

Reader, writer, information and channel are the important components in the communication cycle. The writer perceives information and acts as a generator of information and the same is transmitted through the documentary channel and received by the target audience, the users or readers. For an effective and efficient communication all these components have relational linkages with each other. An attempt is made in this chapter in bringing out how the relationship is expounded among these variables.

## 4.2. READER

Reader or target audience is the ultimate recipient of information. To create an effective document, the writer must know for whom he/she is writing. There are four dimensions to define the reader/user of your document. These include skills, attitude, knowledge and experience(SAKE). What skills do you assume that your reader must have to understand your document? Reader's attitude is almost always a combination of anger and fear. Write with compassion for your reader. In respect of knowledge, what information do you expect the reader to have when they read the document. Skills plus practice, yield experience. Are there any experiences that you expect your readers to have, so that they can understand how to use the document. These four dimensions spell out the word 'SAKE'. This reminds us to write for the sake of our readers.

## 4.3. AUDIENCE ANALYSIS

Audience analysis or reader analysis is a task that is often performed by technical writers in a project's early stages. It consists of assessing the audience to make sure the information relayed to them is at the required level. The audience is often referred as the end-user and all communications need to be targeted towards the defined audience. Defining an audience requires the consideration of many factors such as age, culture and knowledge of the subject. After considering all the known factors, a profile of the intended audience can be created, allowing writers to write in a manner that is understood by the intended audience.

Audience analysis involves gathering and interpreting information about the recipients of oral, written and visual communication. There are numerous methods that a technical communicator can use to conduct the analysis. Because the task of completing an audience analysis can be overwhelming, using a multilayered method to conduct the analysis is recommended by experts, on the basis of accuracy and efficiency. Albers in his study suggested that an analysis use several independent dimensions that work together, such as reader knowledge of the topic and reader cognitive ability. Writers can also use conversation to help them to complete an audience analysis. Bocchi suggests that conversation allows the communicator to consider the multiple cultural, disciplinary, and institutional contexts of their target audience, producing a valuable audience analysis.

David L Carson in a study asserted that technical communicators must function with little to no information to guide them in considering an audience. As a result audience analyses address a fictive audience. He states that to one degree or another, the communicator's image of any particular audience is always a mere figment of imagination. Ideally, the technical communicator would be able to control a project from inception through dissemination. He states that the analysis should include a reader's level of comprehension of the technical vocabulary and motivation, as well as reading level. Indicators of a reader's high level of motivation include high interest in the subject matter, relatively high knowledge of the content, and high personal stakes in mastering the information.

In a study Marjorie Rush Hovde suggests even more tactics that can be implemented in the process of an audience analysis in relation to one's organisation such as talking with users during phone-support calls, interacting with users face-to-face, drawing on the writer's own experiences with the software and documentation, interacting with use-contact people within the organisation, studying responses sent from users after the documentation is released, and conducting user testing.

There are often a large number of factors to consider, thus making it hard for the writer to perfectively assess the target audience within a reasonable amount of time. Therefore, an attempt to reach the most accurate and effective audience analysis, in a timely manner, is vital to the technical communication process. The depth of the audience analysis also depends on the size of the intended audience.

## 4.4. AUDIENCE RESEARCH

Audience research is defined as any communication research that is conducted on specific audience segments to gather information about their attitudes, knowledge, interests, preferences or behaviours.

There are a number of benefits in conducting audience research for effective technical communication. In the initial stages of programme development, exploratory audience research is used to learn about potential audience and the types of incentives and barriers that the audiences perceive exist to adopting a new behaviour (or ceasing an existing one), as well as which incentives and barriers might be addressed effectively by a communication effort. In addition, information often is obtained about the audience's preferred channels or formats of communication, respected or credible sources of information and other issues that programme planners may be considering.

The results from exploratory research are used to create preliminary concepts and /or messages to achieve communications objectives such as increasing knowledge, changing attitudes, enhancing motivation to change behaviours, and increasing the perceived benefits of new behaviours. These concepts then are tested to understand which concept appeals most to the audience and why.

On the basis of the results of concept testing, and before dissemination, the final products such as public service announcements, print advertisements, and education materials- are created and pre tested with individuals from the same audience to ensure that they are understandable and compelling, culturally and linguistically appropriate and supportive of steps to behaviour change.

Audience research also can be used to assess the impact of a communication programme. This research may include testing the target audience concerning awareness of the message, the exposure to or use of the products, or the intention to change behaviour.

## 4.5. READER–WRITER RELATIONSHIP

The relationship between reader and writer is intertwined. Of course, a writer can write without a reader, but if their words remain unread and unexplored, then do the words really mean anything? On the other hand, a reader cannot exist without a writer. Therefore, the relationship is one of symbiosis, a relationship of mutual benefit or dependence.

In scientific communication, there is a pattern of flow of information from generator (writer) to the user(reader). Wherein a quality mechanism exists, there is a built-in-reader-writer relationship. Similarly, in technical writing situations, there is also reader-writer relationship although not so explicit. In addition, reader response, means the behaviour and reactions of users, and feedback mechanism which implies to the way readers express their reactions to the technical document is a normal feature in science communication

Reader response and feedback in technical writing can be assessed indirectly through book reviews, review articles, trend reports, citation analysis etc. In the case of instructional documents one can assess users' responses through questionnaire method. Questions relating to content, structure, style, presentation, understanding, readability and usability can be included in the questionnaire. In the case of operational manuals, performance test that includes pre test and post test can be adopted to assess users' responses. Protocol analysis allows the writer to record readers' responses relating to content, structure, use of jargon, style, organisation of information, comprehensiveness, clarity, precision etc while they read through a document. In the case of investigational reports like commission report, the terms of references form the basis in assessing users' feedback directly through meetings or indirectly through questionnaires. Technical documents such as promotional materials which highlight the features and qualities of information products and services. These promotional materials ensure customer satisfaction effectively and thereby a reader-writer relationship.

For a good technical writing and healthy reader-writer relationship the following tips may be observed by the writers.

- To be good writer, one must form a clear mental picture of the reader and speak to him in an appropriate tone as a real person in a language he/she understands.
- Provide as much context as possible in your writings – historical and cultural, time context etc.
- Anticipate and answer your readers' questions.

- Adopt different modes of presentation – textual and non-textual of information.
- Take your reader on an interesting and well considered journey.
- Respect the time your reader chooses to spend with your writing.

## 4.6. READABILITY AND TEXT

Text readability is a measure of how well and how easily a text conveys its intended meaning to a reader of that text. Easy reading helps learning and enjoyment. So what we write should be easy to understand. Readability is concerned with the issue of matching between the reader and the text. Readability may be defined as reading ease, especially as it results from writing style. Research studies show that easy reading text improves comprehension, retention, reading speed and persistence. Ease of reading, in its turn, is the result of interaction between the text and reader.

Many writers and speakers since ancient times have used plain language. In the 20$^{th}$ century there was much more focus on reading ease. Much of the research has focused on matching texts to people's reading skills. This study has used many successful formulas: in research, government, teaching and publishing. Many people, in many languages, have been helped by these studies. By the year 2000, more than 1000 studies on readability were published in professional journals.

A number of factors influence the readability of a text. These include:

### (i) Physical Factors

There are a number of features not directly related to the reader which may affect readability. Obviously, if the print on the page is difficult to read either because it is too small or the font is an odd one, then this will contribute to reading difficulty.

Clear design and layout is also important and again the reader must be taken into consideration. Typeface, font size, spacing and layout of text are physical factors which influence readability.

### (ii) Reader Factors

The factors affecting readability in relation to readers constitute readers' prior knowledge of the subject, reading skill, interest and motivation. The readers understand more of a text when they know something of the content schema is now well established. It is easy to lose sight of the importance of background knowledge and its effect on readability. Although it is often assumed that writers have particular readers in mind, they may not appreciate the difficulties readers face when there is lack of shared background knowledge. Writers in specialised fields often assume more background knowledge in their readers than is warranted. The reading skill acquired by the reader, reading interest and motivation of a reader in acquiring nascent knowledge can be considered as readability of text in relation to readers.

### (iii) Vocabulary Difficulty

There are so many factors related to vocabulary difficulty to which traditional readability formulae are not sensitive and which may be very complex to investigate. Readability formulae have been criticised for omitting many factors such as syntactic complexity and rhetorical organisation. Studies pointed out that words with three and more syllables known as hard words or difficult words and lengthy sentences affect readability of the text.

### (iv) Text Structure

There is evidence that knowledge of the structure of a text facilitates comprehensibility and recall in investigating both structure and content variables. Thomdyke in a study found that comprehensibility and recall were found to be a function of the amount of inherent plot structure in the story, independent of passage content. Recall probability of individual facts from passages depended on the structural centrality of the facts. In order to facilitate readability consider :

(i) indicating what type of text it is
(ii) summarising main problem and solution or cause and effect
(iii) using graphic organisers to indicate route through the text
(iv) highlighting high level propositions
(v) ensuring that clues of rhetorical organisation are clear
(vi) adding graphical clues such as paragraph indention, numbering, etc.

### (v) Text Coherence and Cohesion

Most readers are aware that some texts, whatever their content, seem better than others and are therefore easier to read. This is a function of how they conform to expectations about text types (rhetorical organisation) but is mainly a function of how they cohere. Coherence normally refers to discourse relations which may or may not be explicitly signalled whereas cohesive devices are surface textual indicators of interconnectiveness. Used well, these devices can greatly contribute to text readability. In order to facilitate readability consider the following tips.

- Highlighting conjunctions or other relation signalling devices.
- Providing questions designed to provoke thought about the relations which hold
- Adding conjunctions of other signalling devices where appropriate
- Making sure that relations which are easily marked
- Replacing pronoun anaphors with more explicit noun anaphors.
- Replacing synonym anaphors with repeated noun
- Where antecedents are distant indicating the connections.
- Checking that where text has been edited anaphor antecedent links are still clear.

- Filling out obscure ellipsis and using repetition rather than substitution.

### (vi) Syntax

Traditional indices estimate text difficulty by measuring sentence length. Considering the effect of syntax, we have similar problem to that of vocabulary correlation and causation. It is clear that long sentences are in general more difficult to understand than short simple ones. However, simplifying a text by reducing syntactic complexity is fraught with difficulty and other clues in meaning may be lost in the process. In order to facilitate readability consider the following.

- Simplifying sentences only as a last resort ensuring that there are no losses of cohesive ties or indicators of intrasentential relations. Restore grammatical cues to structural organisation.
- Using graphical devices to indicate cohesive ties or bridge discontinuities.
- Using inter-linear clues to syntax in the text.

## 4.7. READABILITY INDICES

Attempts to identify factors which affect readability can be traced back a long way. In 1921, Thorndike who examined word frequencies and stared a strand of thought which lives on today in corpus studies. Most subsequent readability formulae have included word frequency and /or word length. The first readability formula was that of Lively and Pressey published in 1923 which was based on vocabulary difficulty. A number of other factors affecting readability have been considered by Vogel and Washburne in 1928. In a study, Gray and Leary published in 1935 listed factors under content, style format and general factors. The best known indices of readability are those of Flesh. The Flesh Reading Ease formula takes into account only words, sentences and syllables. Dalle and Chall in 1948 used two variables such as average sentence length and word familiarity as the indices in their readability formula. Quite a good number of studies were published during 1960s, 1970s, 1980s on readability indices for and against in the choice of variables used in readability formula. Davison and Kantor (1982)in their study remarked that 'objections may be made to readability formula in general. Reading difficulty may be affected by the purposes and background of the reader and the inherent difficulties of the subject matter; it is not just a function of measurable properties like length and vocabulary'

A study conducted by Harrison(1980) points out how comprehension tests have been used as a basis for deriving readability formulae. Readability is an attribute of text, while comprehension is an attribute of readers. There is fundamental difference between the two concepts. However, at the same time, these concepts are intimately related with each other, in that estimating readability is a matter of predicting the extent of the reader's comprehension of a text.

According to Schema Theory (Armbruster, 1986), knowledge is stored in the memory in terms of content and textual schemas. Content schemas contain knowledge about objects, events and situations while textual schemas contain knowledge about the conventions of organised discourse. Textual schemas include knowledge about discourse structures that are common to most forms of text such as paragraphs, as well as specialised discourse structures such as those for stories or scientific article. Readers comprehend a text when they are able to bring to mind schemas that match the particular content and structure of the material. As they begin to read, readers search for a schema to account for the information in the text. Here there is meaning anticipation and contextual predictability in the reader. On the basis of the schema, readers construct a partial tentative model of the text meaning.

This model provides a framework continuing the search through the text. The model is progressively refined as the readers gather more information from the text. Reading comprehension thus involves the progressive refinement of a coherent model of the text's meaning. The Schema theory therefore states that meaning does not reside in the text alone, but is a product of the interaction of reader and text. On the basis of reading comprehension tests, the norms for the readability formulae have been formulated.

## 4.8. READABILITY FORMULAE

A good number of readability formulae have been developed by linguists and researchers to measure the readability of the text. Some of the popular readability formulae are the Automated Readability Index, Flesch Reading Ease, Gunning Fog Index, Modified Fog Index, Cloze Test etc. The formulae are widely used to match texts with the reading level of the audience. The readability of the text calculated based on Modified Fog Index (MFI) is illustrated with a passage taken from a text given below.

> [The human language faculty is thought to be fundamentally different from and of much higher complexity than those of other species. Human language is highly complex in that it is based on a set of rules relating symbols to their meanings, thereby forming an infinite number of possible innovative utterances from a finite number of elements. Language is thought to have originated when early hominids first stated cooperating, adapting earlier systems of communication based on expressive signs to include a theory of other minds and shared intentionality. This development is thought to have coincided with an increase in brain volume]

**Steps**

1. The above passage consists of 100 words
2. Now, find the average length of complete sentences in the text by dividing the total number of words with total number of sentences. ie 100/4 = 25
3. Count the number of words with three or more syllables(difficult words)from the passage. The answer is 23
4. Now calculate Modified Fog Index( MFI) formula

$$\frac{2(ASL + DW)}{5} + 5$$

Here ASL = average sentence length and DW = total number of difficult words

i.e., $\frac{2(25 + 23)}{5} + 5 = \frac{2(48)}{5} + 5 = \frac{96}{5} + 5$

= 19.2 + 5

= 24,2 : This is the readability score

The score can be interpreted as follows:

12 and below : very easy text

13–16 : easy text

17–20 : quite difficult text

over 20 : very difficult text

From the above calculation it is inferred that the passage taken from the text is very difficult.

Another formula for estimation is Flesch Formula. The same passage used for estimation of Modified Fog Index can be used to estimate Flesch Formula.

Reading ease score = 206.835

- (0.846 x SYLLS/100w)

- (1.015 x WDS/SEN)

Here Syll/100 + Total syllables per 100 words + average number of words per sentence

## Steps

1. Count 100 words from the passage
2. Now find the average length of sentences i.e 100/4 = 25
3. Count the total number of syllables in 100 words = 171
4. Now apply the Flesch Formula

   206.835– (0.846 x 171) – (1.015 x 25)

206.835 – (144.666) – (25.375)

206.835 -170.035 = 36.794

5. The score is 36.794.

From the score, 36.794 calculated as per formula it is inferred that since the score value is less than 50 the sample passage from the text taken is very difficult. The score value also corroborates the findings arrived from the Modified Fog Index.

## REFERENCES

Alber, Michael J.(2003). Multidimensional audience analysis for dynamic information. Journal of Technical Writing and Communication. 33. PP263-279.

Armbruster, BB(1986). Schema theory and the design of content area of text books. Educational Psychologist.24(4).pp 253-267.

Bocchi, Joseph S(1991). Forming constructs of audience convention, conflict and conversation. Jl.of Business and Technical Communication.5. pp.151-172.

Chall, JS( 1958). Readability: An appraisal of research and application. Columbus Bureau of Educational Research. Ohio State University.

Dale, E and Chall, JS (1948) A formula for predicting readability. Educational Research Bulletin.. 27.pp 11-20.

Flesch,R (1948) A new readability yardstick. Jl.of Applied Psychology. 32.pp.221-233

Harrison, C(1980) Readability in the classroom. Cambridge, Cambridge University Press.

Hovde, Marjorie Rush(2000). Tactics for building images of audience in organisational contexts. Jl.of Business and Technical Communicaiton.14. pp395-444.

Jenkins, J (1987). Course development: A manual for editors of distance – teaching materials. Cambridge, International Extension college.

Taylor, W (1953). Cloze procedure: A new tool for measuring readability. Journalism Quarterly. 30.pp414-438.

Wikipedia, the Free Encyclopedia.

# 5

# Aberrations in Technical Writing

## 5.1. INTRODUCTION

An aberration is something that deviates from the normal way. In technical writing the deviation of any sort from the normal situation will defeat the real objective of the communication. The success of communication depends on transmission of information or ideas from the communicator to the communicatee. In any stages of technical writing process aberration may happen which may lead to the weakness to any form of technical document. An aberrant technical document results due to insufficient or inaccurate content, weak organisation of information, careless use of language, poor documentation and inappropriate or inaccurate visuals. Also such a document results in deficiency in communicating its purpose to transmit the information to the target audience. In fact, a technical document may be well written and complete in coverage, but ineffective or weak if the needs of the target audience are left unsatisfied.

## 5.2. FACTORS OF ABERRATION

Aberrations in technical writing may occur mainly due to factors like content reliability, weak organisation of information, careless use of language, poor documentation, inaccurate visuals and technical style of presentation.

**Content Reliability**

Content reliability is ensured by accuracy, preciseness and completeness of the information contained in the document.

A technical document is prepared in various stages – from the time it is started to its final production. A technical writer, apart from scheduling his tasks and setting, draws up an outline or plan to ensure cohesion and coherence of the content and to see that it meets the requirements and specifications. The technical writer should revise and check at each stage of the writing in order to produce a faultless document. For eliminating errors technical writer should prepare checklists for each stage of writing. The checklists may include aspects like specification for the document, target readership, availability of various types of information sources, outline contains all the necessary features of the document etc.

The purpose of technical writing is to instruct, to persuade or to inform. It is the responsibility of the writer to ensure that the document is reliable, complete, accurate and precise. This means that all relevant statements should be supported by evidence which is substantiated and well documented. The value of technical document correlates positively with the accuracy, completeness and precision of information it contains and its relevance to the target audience. A reliable document is generated by the writer through awareness and exploitation of various types of sources of information, organisation of content, use of visuals and documentation. Any error in these aspects would lead the document weak or faulty and in need of correction.

The reliability of a text is directly related to the accuracy and completeness of the information contained in the document. If the writer has insufficient grasp of the data or the subject under study he will not be able to write an accurate and complete text. So the reliability of the information depends on the extent and depth of the study undertaken by the writer. Unless the various information sources both documentary and non-documentary are not used effectively by the writer. They may lead to inaccurate and incomplete information in the text. There are sources of information such as personal observation and activities, calculations, samples and specimens, experiments, internal records, current versions of documents, document testing, interviews and letters of inquiry, surveys and polls, library sources, computerised databases and government documents as listed by Rebecca and Burnett(1990) in Technical communication. The writer can select any source/s out of these depending upon the nature and purpose of the subject demands and requirements of the target audience. In the selection of the sources, what is needed is proper evaluation to ensure the quality of its content. It is evident that content- wise a text can be aberrant, that is incomplete or inaccurate, if the writer has poor grasp of the subject and inadequate support and documentation. Also the completeness of information in a text has also to be matched against the requirements of targeted audience.

## Organisation of Information

Once the information is collected and selected, it needs to be organised and presented as a text that can be easily read, understood and assimilated by the target audience. The organisation of information adopted may be logical, chronological, psychological or topical. In its turn, organisation of information in a text brings clarity. If the text lacks clarity it may be due to the failure of the author to organise the material properly and present information in logical order. The technical writer should understand the principles of organising text in the expository writing and various formats of technical documents. In the expository writing, the body or text should have a beginning as introduction followed by theme of the study and finally summary of the findings, conclusion and recommendations. In the introduction the writer should introduce the topic under study, purpose and relevance of the study, statement of the problem etc. The body or text should contain analysis and discussion and interpretation while the conclusion should summarise the important findings, conclusions and recommendations. Besides, organisation adopted is dependent on the formats of various forms of technical document. The formats are more or less standardised but variations may occur. The format of an instruction manual is different from a commission report while the format of a commission report is different from a research report like thesis. In the case of a thesis the format consists of three areas viz preliminaries, the text and auxiliaries that are in order. In the first part, preliminaries consist of title page, certificate, declaration, acknowledgement, contents page, list of tables, list of figures, list of appendices, list of abbreviations etc. The second part is the text or the body of the thesis logically organised under various chapters under the headings Introduction, Review of related studies, back ground chapter relating to the subject, analysis and discussion of the collected data and final chapter contains findings, conclusion and recommendation. The third part of the thesis is the auxiliaries containing appendices, bibliography, glossary and index etc. In the case of an instruction manual the format consists of title, introduction, target audience, theory of operation, training section, instruction, maintenance and user's guide.

The technical writer should ensure consistency of terminology used in the text. The use of synonym and near synonyms is not approved in technical writing. The technical writer should also ensure that logical linking of information by sentence by sentence, paragraph by paragraph, section by section for a cohesive organisation of information of the document. Any deviation from the above aspects relating to the organisation of information in the document may lead to its weakness and failure in successful communication.

### Visual Aids

Application of Visual aides or non-textual presentation is one of the important characteristic features of technical document. Visual aides like tables, charts, graphs, diagrams, flowcharts, drawings, photographs etc are used when ideas and concepts in a text are complex and too abstract for the target reader. Errors may occur some time in the use of visual aids which may lead to aberration of the document. Use of visuals in inappropriate place is one such situation. Lack of appropriate headings to the visuals, lack of serial number to each visual, lack of linking of the visuals with matter in the text etc cause aberration of the document. Errors in the mathematical scales used for charts, graphs etc cause aberration. In certain situations, terms like ' table above' 'table below' or graph above, graph below etc placed wrongly lead to confusion to the reader. So avoid the use of terms 'above' and 'below', instead use table number or figure number 1, 2,3 etc for linking the textual matter with visual aids.

### Documentation

Quite a good number of information sources may be used by the technical writer in the form of ideas, quotation, illustration etc in the technical document. It is imperative that all these sources used should be documented with complete references and acknowledged. Incomplete references may be in the form of incomplete imprint statement, incomplete quotations, wrong page number of the cited document etc. While documenting the information sources, the technical writer should not deviate from the standard systems of documentation. Style manuals like The Chicago Style Manual, Modern Language Association(USA) Handbook or catalogue codes like CCC, AACR etc may be used for documentation for consistency and standardisation of the citations. Incomplete documentation leads to the weakness of the technical document.

### Technical Style

The core of the activity in the writing of the technical document is a style that is easily understood and is pleasing to the target audience. The style that is universally recommended focuses on accuracy, brevity, clarity and readability. Accuracy in style results from precise use of terms and proper sentence structure.

Precision in expression would eliminate redundancy leading to clarity and brevity. There will be brevity and clarity by the maximum use of technical terms and formal standardised sentence structure.

Diction is the use of words and phrases in a particular context giving a distinctive quality. The words function to make the meaning immediately clear. Diction in technical writing means being aware of certain dos and don'ts in the use of words and phrases for the purpose of clarity. The use of technical words is an essential feature of technical diction. Technical terms are necessary as they identify precisely an idea or an object. Their use makes the writing economical and to the point and they help in quick communication.

The technical writer can avoid falling into the jargon trap and ensure proper diction by the practice of simple rules in the choice of words and phrases. He should be beware of lengthy terms(difficult words or words with more than three syllables) made up of noun strings. He should check writing to avoid repetition of terms, phrases and ideas which leads to redundancy. He should prefer positive to negative phrasing.

Grammatical errors occurring in a technical document also lead to the weakness of a document. Technical writers should make use of active voice rather than passive voice. The active voice form gives a sentence directness and makes it shorter and easier to read without loss of meaning. In the use of modifiers, modifiers should be placed as close as possible to the word they modify. If the modifier is so placed in a sentence that it does not modify the subject of a sentence, it is called dangling modifiers. It is well known rule of grammar that subject and verb should agree in number and person. Yet this is an area of frequent mistakes. In the use of pronouns, these should refer to nouns already stated and should be as close to their antecedents as possible. Loss of meaning will result if the reference is remote, missing or vague. When ideas or facts of equal importance are to be stated in a sentence the writer should use equivalent grammatical structures for proper emphasis. Parallel constructions should be joined by and, but, or, not only, but also, both, either or, neither nor etc.

Correct use of punctuation is another aspect to be considered in technical communication. Careless use of punctuation can be a cause of aberration. Punctuations marks like colon, semi colon, dash, parenthesis, quotation mark, apostrophe, coma, full stop etc are used in language. Colon is used as a convention in citations; in titles; in salutations ; to set of long quotations; and in a sentence to introduce a list or a series. Semi colon is used to link two closely related sentences while dash is used when the definition of a term within a sentence needs to be separated from its main idea. Parenthesis is used to separate supplementary information, such as technical terms, within a sentence. Quotation marks are used to indicate the titles of articles from journals etc while apostrophe is used to form the possessive. Coma is used in dates, numbers, informal salutations, and titles or degree while Full stop is used to indicate the end of a sentence.

The careful use of abbreviations, numerals, capitals, hyphenated words, quotation marks etc is another aspect to be considered by the writer in documentation. Technical writer should be aware of an error or weakness in any of these areas which would make a text aberrant. Abbreviations speed up actual writing itself as they function like a code or short form system. A technical document writing frequently expresses information in quantitative terms using numerals. In such case it can be expressed in the most comprehensible manner, using words if necessary.

The above discussion brings out the following guidelines or principles in respect of the technical style of presentation of information in technical writing.

- Use language that ensures precision, brevity, clarity and readability;
- Avoid jargon or use it sparingly
- Use simple, direct, specific and concrete words instead of general abstract words and phrases

- Avoid noun strings, redundant terms and negative phrasing
- In relation to grammatical structures, use active voice instead of passive voice
- Punctuation marks used should be consistent and appropriate
- Use conventional abbreviations, numerals, capitals, quotation marks in documentation.

## REFERENCES

Burnett, R.E (1990) Technical communication. California, Wadsworth Publishing.

Cooper, B.M( 1964) Writing technical report. London Penguin Books.

Evans, J( 1983) Beginner's Guide to technical writing. London, Butterworth.

Ewer, J and Latorre ( 1969) A course in basic scientific English. London, Longman.

Gravey, WD(1979) Communication: the essence of science facilitating information exchange among libraries, scientists and students. Oxford, Pergamon Press.

Gunning, R (1963) New Guide to more effective writing in business and industry. Boston, Industrial Education Institute.

Pauley, SE (1979) Technical report writing. Boston, Houghton Mifflin.

# 6

# Organistion of Data/ Information In Various Technical Documents

## 6.1. INTRODUCTION

Data is the collective recording of information, either numerical or otherwise. Data can be classified into various ways. It can be classified based on measurability as quantitative data and qualitative data. While, data can be classified based on the collection procedure as :

- Primary data
- Secondary data
- Tertiary data.

Data is collected during scientific investigations which need to be transformed into some format that allows interpretation and analysis between the variables. In fact, any data collected in research is always in an unorganised form and needs to be organised and presented in a meaningful and readily comprehensible form in order to facilitate further analysis and interpretation. The collected data can be presented in the following ways.

Classification of the data is the process of grouping entities according to their resemblances or similarities. The grouping of entities can be based on chronological, geographical, qualitative attributes such as sex, literacy, religion etc and quantitative attributes like height, weight, age, income etc. The classified data can be presented in tabular form. Tabulation is the process of summarising classified data in the form of tables that are systematically arranged in columns and rows. Data in the form of diagrammatic presentation such as charts, graphs, figures etc is another form of representation.

In the presentation of information an important aspect to be considered is the subject of the document. Depending on the nature of information of the subject concerned, an appropriate presentation is chosen. Another aspect which influences the form of presentation relates to the type of information products. The type of presentation is also influenced by the type of users to whom it is meant. For a manager who is tight in time would prefer non-textual presentation with minimum textual presentation. While, R & D scientists would prefer textual presentation with necessary illustrations. In the case of extension workers they are comfortable with illustrative manuals and guides than fully text-oriented manuals and guides. These factors reveal that the parameters to be considered in the design of an effective presentation are users, purpose or impact wished on the user, subject, product and media of communication.

## 6.2. ORGANISATION OF INFORMATION IN VARIOUS TYPES OF TECHNICAL COMMUNICATION

The following sections deal with organisation of information in various types of technical documents such as abstract, popular article, technical article, dissertation and thesis, project proposal, house journal, audio-visual presentation and website.

### 6.21. Organisation of information in Abstract

An abstract is defined as a summarised, accurate

representation of the significant content of a document. It is usually accompanied by an adequate bibliographical description to enable the original document to be traced. In fact, an abstract is thus a document surrogate. Other types of document surrogates are abridgment, annotation, extract, excerpt, summary, synopsis, précis etc. Mikhailov and Giliyarevski have defined abstract as ' An abstract is a summary of a document, specifying its nature as well as the techniques, findings, time and place of an investigation; it also indicates the objective and main theoretical premises of a study, supplies the pertinent figures, formulae, tables, charts and diagrams and conclusions with the number of illustrations, tables, charts, diagrams and reference in the abstract publication, as well as the abstractor's name'

In respect of uses academic literature uses the abstract to succinctly communicate complex research. An abstract may act as a stand-alone entity instead of a full paper. As such, an abstract is used by many organisations as the basis for selecting research that is proposed for the presentations in various forms. Most literature database search engines index only abstracts rather than providing the entire text of the paper.

## Types of Abstracts

The abstracts can be categorised on the basis of the information content of the abstract and on the basis of the generator who prepares it. They are :

**Titular Abstract :** It is also known as title only abstract as the title is used to describe the contents of a document.

**Indicative abstract :** Information pertaining to the subject of a document provided indicatively is known as indicative abstract. It can provide only clues about the information content of a document It is also known as descriptive abstract.

**Micro-abstract :** Micro abstract or mini abstract is highly condensed indicative abstract. CA Condensates is an example that provides mini abstract.

**Informative abstract** : Informative abstract is also known as comprehensive abstract or abstract-synopsis It provides a concise summary of the significant contributions made by the document in the field of knowledge. Informative abstract serves as an adequate substitute for the original document. The average length of an informative abstract ranges 200-300 words.

**Indicative-informative abstract** : This type of abstract provides the qualities of both indicative and informative abstracts in relation to the abstracting of the content of a document. Some of the areas in the contents of a document are prepared indicatively and some of the areas in the document are abstracted informatively on the basis of the user's requirement. So, it is also known as slanted abstract.

**Graphic Abstract** : In the field of Chemistry where a precise language of communication is available, a new type of abstract has been introduced in Current abstract of Chemistry. This has been named graphic abstract. Instead of naming the substances and compounds and their treatments, a graphic abstract indicates them by molecular and structural formulae.

**Telegraphic Abstract** : Telegraphic abstract is also known as standardised or encoded abstract. It is a detailed index to a graphic record which is composed of significant words selected from the documents; code symbols called role indicators supply a context for the selected words; and punctuation symbols which separate and group the words and role indicators into various units in a somewhat the same fashion as conventional punctuation does.

**Auto- Abstract** : Auto-abstract is a computer generated abstract. It is produced by the computer on the basis of the frequency of the use of significant words in a document and the frequency with which these high frequency words appear in the same sentence in which they occurred and their position noted. A score is then assigned to each sentence based on the number and position of the high frequency words it contains. In fact auto-abstract is a collection of the most informative sentences from the original document.

**Author Abstract**: Author abstract is prepared by the author and it forms part of the. original article. The abstract may be indicative or informative abstract which is usually governed by the editorial policy of the journal in which it is given.

## Abstracting

Abstracting is the process of making abstract. An abstract should be self -contained. It would be expected to reveal the essential features of the original document. The abstracting work constitutes the following three stages.

In the first stage the abstractor should identify the significant or key terms from the various parts of the document to be abstracted. The areas to be scanned for the identification of the significant terms are author abstract, introductory part, methodology part, summary of finding regions of the document. The second stage of abstracting work is to organise the ideas or significant terms that are selected in the first stage. These ideas or key terms should be organised in the sequence: i) purpose or objective, ii) methodology, techniques and instruments, iii)results and iv) conclusion. The third stage in abstracting is to prepare the abstract in accurate and precise manner.

In the writing of the abstract, all rules applicable to language, grammar and style should be followed. To achieve the best result is to remember the tips relating to technical writing. The abstract should be prepared in easy-to-read prose. Phrases such as 'the paper deals with or the 'paper briefly discusses' may be avoided. It is desirable to use short sentences. Avoid repetition of the title. Technical jargon, abbreviations, symbols and trade names may be used with discretion. Past tense is to be used to describe the specific activities that the author is reporting, since these are already in the past. But the conclusions that he/she draws from these activities though hold true in the present they are to be written in the past tense. Maximum economy is to be ensured in the use of words. The abstract should be consistent in tone and emphasis with the document being abstracted. Use standardised terminology. In regard to length of abstract, 200-300 words for informative or critical abstract and about 50 words for indicative abstract.

**Organisation of data/Information in Abstract**

The anatomy of abstract reveals the organisation of information in abstract. An example from Indian Science Abstract, July 2011 is given below to illustrate the anatomy of abstract.

O13171 LEMJ P. TRIPATHY D P (Mining Engineering Dep, PNG Technology Univ.LAE Morobe Province 411, Papau New Guinea. E mail: debitrivathy@yahoo.co.in) : Environmental impacts of disposal of mining wastes and mill tailings in Papua New Guinea(PNG) mines – an overview. Pollut. Res 2009, 28(1), 1-12.

{CITATION PART}

Papua New Guinea being a major producer of gold and copper, has three world class and two medium-scale gold and copper mines most of which have life of more than ten(10) years. These mines though contribute two-thirds of country's GDP but produce a lot of mine and mill wastes that are not properly controlled. Paupa New Guinea mines have a record of poor waste management since the mine and mill wastes do not have permanent impoundments. The mill wastes are discharged directly to the river systems or ocean whereas the mine waste rocks that are dumped at temporary sites on the surface also finds their way to the water systems through surface run-off. These wastes are directly disposed to the environment through riverine or marine tailings disposals. The water where the mine residues enters are tainted with toxic materials such as cyanide and high level of heavy metal ins rendering it unsafe for drinking and washing. Most people living along the affected areas are also contaminated but are taking time to show out. Huge volume of mill tailings and mine wastes rocks that are disposed annually at an alarming rate also give rise to high sedimentation problem. Reverine or deep sea wastes disposal systems have been granted by the government much in favour of the developers. Such wastes management systems in developed countries like Australia, United Kingdom, USA and Canada are highly forbidden because they can adversely affect the environment. In Papua New Guinea mines, the developers who come from these developed countries, however, employ reverine and marine tailings disposal while putting much emphasis on the rugged terrain and high rainfall experienced in the country. This paper discusses in detail the present status of environmental impacts of different waste disposal practices in some of the base metal mines of Papua New Guinea e.g.OK Tedi, Lihir, Tolukuma and Pogera mines and their management for ensuring the sustainable development of the mining industry. It is felt by the authors that it would have been better if the government of Papua New Guinea had not allowed mining to go ahead with such wastes disposal practices than to face the mess mining activities have created. The economic gains of the country are becoming less significant with the massive pollution at bay. It is felt that proper disposal and management of mine wastes and mill tailings in Papua New Guinea have to be planned prior to commencement of mining, in the developmental stage and continuously applied and improved throughout the existing life of the projects to ensure minimum environmental impacts. 18 illus, 2 tables, 15 ref.

{ABSTRACT PART}

The above record consists of two distinct regions: Citation and abstract part. The citation comprises name of the author, title of the article, name of the journal in which the article is published, volume number, issue number, year and pagination. The organisation of information in abstract part constitutes the purpose, methodology, results and conclusion in order.

## 6.22. Organisation of Information in Popular Article

Popular article is usually written for general public as a light reading material for information. Topics of contemporary significance to the general public are taken for writing Topics such as 'Information literacy', 'smallness of libraries', whither books ?, 'E-waste', 'community colleges', 'Internet', Reading and electronic media etc can be taken as subjects for writing popular articles. Popular articles are usually published in popular periodicals and news papers.

In the preparation of popular articles the following are some of the parameters.

In respect of length, these are shorter articles providing broader overviews of topics discussed. In-depth analysis is to be avoided. Popular articles are not usually written by subject specialist. Staff writers and journalists write popular articles. Readers or target audience constitute lay people, folks without higher qualifications. In fact, any one who can read and write are target audience. In the case of language, non-technical language accessible to generally knowledgeable audience is used in popular article. Popular articles do not necessarily follow specific format or structure. In the case of special features, illustrations mainly with glossy or colour photographs are used. While in scholarly articles illustrations support the text. A bibliography is not provided, although names of reports or references may be mentioned in the text. Popular articles are not evaluated and peer reviewed.

Evan Kelly has given ten steps in writing popular articles. They are :

- Aim to be interesting, polished and informative
- Remove your limits

Reduce your subject to a single core word and then brainstorm around it. For example, if you are trying to write about 'study skills' expand your thinking to 'school'. Now jot down everything that comes to mind when you think about school, and when you run out of ideas start asking yourself open questions around the subject and noting your answers.

**Restore your focus :** Once you have started to understand the general feelings of your readers, allow your mind to focus back on your original topic of 'study skills'. From your new perspective, what questions would you ask?

**Be your audience :** Write each question on a separate sheet of paper; do not stop until you have at least ten and preferably more. Stay in the mindset of your readers until you feel you have asked every major questions that concern them.

**Take a step back :** Put your pile of questions aside for a few hours, overnight if possible. Don't consciously think about them. Give your subconscious time to process them without any further prompting from you.

**Get out of your pen and write :** When you are ready, sit down with pages of questions and simply start to answer them. Writing your answers by hand can give you access to ideas that might be missed if you type them.

**Edit lightly :** Trust first instincts. Proof –read and correct any obvious errors, but don't do any major editing until your piece has had time to sit for a while. Again, leaving it overnight will give you a fresh perspective the next time you look at it.

**Polish it up :** Short articles are unlikely to need major editing if you have written them as described here. They will follow easily and naturally already and having each question and answer on a separate sheet makes it easier to select only the ones you want. Your job now is to put them in a reasonably logical sequence and make sure they are understandable and that the reader is led smoothly from one question and answer to the next.

**Top and tail it :** Write a brief introductory paragraph as a 'teaser' for the main article. Many article directories now put the first paragraph of each piece into RSS feeds which are picked up by other web sites. So you want to make sure two or three major key words appear at least once in that first paragraph. Write another short paragraph to summarise the major points of the article and provide some ideas for the reader to explore the subject further.

**Submit it** : Distribute your article to directories, special interest group and publishers.

Mark A Abrahams has suggested six simple steps for writing popular articles. They are:

**Step 1 – Choose a highly targeted market** : You need to focus on writing your article for a specific audience that will read it. Usually this will mean writing an article to solve a specific problem

**Step 2- Write your introduction and conclusion first** : Write your introduction and conclusion first as this allows you to get your creative juices flowing so that you can write the body of the article which is the toughest.

**Step 3- Create bullet points for your body** : Brainstorm ideas for your specific topic and write these ideas as bullet points and then expand on each idea. You will find that it is much easier to expand on your bullet points than to immediately write sentences about your topic.

**Step -4 Proof your article** : Once you have written your article you need to check it for spelling and grammatical errors.

**Step-5 Write a summary** : You need to create a summary for your article which will describe it in a few sentences. This is important for article directories that will list your title and summary with a link to your article.

**Step – 6 Submit your article** : This step is intended for the publication of the article.

## 6.23.Organisation of Information in Technical Article/ Research Paper

The purpose of research is to increase the store of human knowledge, and so even the very best work is useless if you cannot effectively communicate it to the rest of the world. Writing technical article or research paper will clarify your thinking and thereby improve your research potential. You can present your findings in a professional gathering, or if you wish to reach a wider audience. You can publish your work in a scholarly journal. An organised and analytical study of a given subject written mainly to record and disseminate information is known as technical paper or research paper.

## Characteristics

In its style, structure, and approach, a technical article closely resembles a formal report. Meenakshi Raman and Sangeetha Sharma have suggested the following characteristics of a research paper.

i) A research paper is the most important form of expository discourse. It may be written on any topic or subject – scientific, technical, social, cultural etc but the treatment is scholarly in nature

ii) It is highly stylised and contains a high concentration of certain writing techniques such as definition, classification, interpretation, abstraction, description etc.

iii) It is objective in nature and the presentation of information is accurate, concise, direct, and unambiguous.

iv) Generally, it contains almost all those formal elements which a technical report includes.

v) Most research papers are characterised by the use of graphic aids, and scientific, technical, or specialised vocabulary.

vi) Every research paper is unified composition arising out of the study of a particular subject, assembling the relevant data, and organising and analysing the same.

vii) A research paper is a documented prose work. All important analyses have to be supported by adequate evidence. In short, documentation is essential for all research papers.

## Factors to be considered for writing technical Article

Michael Ernst has suggested the following factors to be considered by the technical writer while writing a technical paper.

**Know your message, and stay on message** : Before you write your paper, you need to understand your audience and your message. Who will read it, and what are the key points you want that person to take away from it? Once you know this, then you can organise the paper to support exactly those points and to eliminate irrelevant detail. Determine your goal and focus the paper around that goal. Write for the readers, rather than writing for yourself. Your paper needs to convince the audience of three key points: that the problem is interesting, that it is hard, and that you solved it. If any of these is missing or unclear, the paper will not be compelling. For each point in your paper, you need to explain both what and why. Do not write your paper as a chronological narrative of all the things that you tried, and do not devote space in the paper proportionately to the amount of time you spent on each task. The audience is interested in what worked, and why, so start with that. You need to convince your readers that your contributions are novel.

**Make the organisation and results clear :** A paper should communicate the main ideas of your research early and clearly. Then, the body of the paper can expand on these points; a reader who understands the structure and big ideas can better appreciate the details. For each section of the paper, consider writing a mini introduction that says what its organisation is, what is in each part, and how the parts relate to one another.

**Brevity :** Be brief. Make every word count. If a word does not support your point, cut it out, because excess verbiage and fluff only make it harder for the reader to appreciate your message. Use shorter and more direct phrases wherever possible. Make your writing crisp and to the point.

**Writing Style :** Passive voice has no place in technical writing. It obscures who the actor was, what caused it, and when it happened. Use active voice and simple, clear, direct phrasing. First person is rarely appropriate. First person should never be used to describe the operation of a programme or system. Avoid puffery, self congratulation, and value judgement: give the facts and let the reader judge. Do not use words like 'obviously' or 'clearly'. Prefer singular to plural number. When describing an experiment or some other action that occurred in the past, use past tense. Avoid gratuitous use of the future tense 'will'.

**Figures :** Use figures! Different people learn in different ways, so you should complement a textual or mathematical presentation with a graphical one. Figures can also help to illustrate concepts, draw a skimming reader into the text, and make the paper more visually appealing.

**Naming :** Give each concept in your paper a descriptive name. Avoid acronyms when possible. It is better to name a technique based on what it does rather than how it does it. Use terms consistently and precisely. Do not use a single term to refer to multiple concepts.

**Feedback :** Get feedback! Finish your paper well in advance, so that you can improve the writing. Even re-reading your own text after being away from it can show you things that you did not notice. Some of your best feedback will be from yourself, especially as you get more thoughtful and introspective about your writing.

**Related works:** A related work section should not only explain what research others have done, but in each case should compare and contrast that to your work. After reading your related work section, a reader should understand the key idea and contribution of each significant piece of related work, and how your work differs.

## The Format or Structure of a Technical Article

The format of a technical article comprises : Preliminaries, The body and Auxiliaries.

The preliminaries consist of the following components or elements

**Title :** The title of a technical paper is the coextensive treatment of the content of the paper. It should not be too short or too long. Use specific terms rather than general terms in the title.

If the main title does not express adequately the content of the document, sub-title can be used

**Author/s statement** : The name of the author/s with designation and mailing address /s is given here. E-mail address can also be given for communication between authors and readers.

**Abstract with key terms** : The abstract is the precise summary of the paper. It enables the reader to identify the basic content of the document quickly. It also enables to meet the requirements of the abstracting periodicals. Normally, the informative abstract contains all important aspects such as purpose, methods and materials, results and conclusion. It should be concise and self-contained. The abstract is followed with significant terms or key words that represent the various facets of the content of the document for retrieval.

### The Main Body

The main body of the technical paper consists of the following

**Introduction** : The purpose of introduction is to introduce the topic to the readers, This enables to supply sufficient background information so as to allow the reader to understand and evaluate the results of the study.

Nature and scope of the problem studied and relevance in selecting such a topic for investigation can also be given in this area.

**Materials and Methods** : The main purpose of this section is to describe the experimental technique, experimental design or theoretical derivation. For materials, relevant specification must be given. Experiments performed, the ranges covered, the new equipment used etc should be described in detail.

**Results** : This section is the data analysis and presentation section which is the core of the technical paper. The presentation of data may be in three ways: textual presentation, non-textual presentation and illustrative presentation. The textual presentation is descriptive form of presentation of the data. While non-textual presentation is in the form of tables, charts, graphs etc. The illustrative presentation of the data may be in the form of figures, photographs etc.

**Discussion :** The main function of this section is to interpret data and to highlight the significant features of the data and the possible causes of these features.

**Conclusion :** The conclusions of the paper should stem from the data presented and no extra material should be introduced. When there are significant findings, conclusions are necessary part of the paper. Recommendations or suggestions can also be included in the light of the results obtained in the study.

**Auxiliaries**

The auxiliaries consist of the following components

**Acknowledgements :** Acknowledgements usually follow the main body of the article.

The writer should acknowledge in this section any significant help he/she received from any individual, institution etc. Acknowledgements can also be given to any funding agency for awarding grants as fellowship for the conduct of the study.

**Appendices :** Appendices in the form of questionnaire, interview schedules and other long list of materials referred in the textual area are provided in this section with appendix number and headings.

**List of abbreviations and symbols :** This section contains list of abbreviations along with standard expansion. Standard expansion of the symbols used in the text is also provided in this section.

**References :** The studies cited in the textual area are provided here as references. The references should be complete in all respects. References taken from second hand sources should not be cited in technical paper. In the case of a journal article, the reference constitutes the elements such as name of the author, title of the article, abbreviated name of the journal in which the article is published, volume number, issue number, year and pagination. Standard format followed in style manuals can be used in the preparation of the references.

## 6.25. Organisation of Information in Research Reports – Dissertation/Thesis

Communication of result through research report is an important aspect of any research activity. Thus while reporting, scholars have scientific obligation to effectively communicate about completed investigation in a comprehensive and accurate manner. The utility of research lies in its wider dissemination and hence it is obligatory for the researchers to communicate their results of research in a systematic manner. The production of meaningful and effective research report depends on the writing skill of the researcher and his ability to use suitable visual techniques.

Research report writing is the culmination of the research investigation. It is at this stage of reporting that the researcher assembles the findings of the study, draws conclusions and evaluates his own findings. Report writing is thus the end product of research activity. Writing a research report is a technical activity which demands all the skills and patience from the researcher. It requires considerable thought, effort, patience and an overall approach to the problem, data, analysis as well as firm control over language and greater objectivity. To write the report, a vast amount of planning and preparation is necessary.

Besides, perfection in the research report can be achieved only by continuous and persistent thought and creative and intelligent writing.

The production of an effective report depends on a combination of factors such as the ability and skill of the investigators for analysis, synthesis and exposition. The major components of effective report writing are the following :

- Selection of an appropriate reader population
- Major components of completed research reports
- Fundamentals of style and grammar; and
- Preparation of manuscripts.

**Selection of an appropriate population**

A research report is meant for several categories of audiences viz scientists engaged in fundamental research, those engaged in applied research, practitioners, policy makers, funding agencies and the general public. The report should focus on the target audience and include the material of interest to other audience only if it does not interfere with the material required by the specific audience.

**Dissertation and Thesis**

Dissertation/Thesis is a report or treatise prepared as a part of an academic course for a higher degree or diploma. In India, the project report prepared as part of an academic programme diploma or Master's degree is termed as dissertation and the report prepared for doctoral degree and above is termed as thesis. While the terminologies dissertation and thesis used in the USA is just reverse. Dissertation and thesis differ in respect of intention and extension of the subject under research.

**Writing the Research Report**

Utmost attention should be paid for writing the research report. The report is a communication between the researcher and the reader. The report should be clear, easy to read and accurate in information and statements. Vagueness and generalization will make the report incomplete. The essence of communication is clarity in presentation. The following points should be borne in mind while writing the research report.

- Clear thinking and clear presentation of the report are important aspects. Poor writing is largely due to hazy thinking. Research report writing is a reasoning process and without clarity of thought, there will not be clarity in writing.

- The researcher should have a good command over language. Too frequently faulty sentence structure, illogical paragraphing, poor punctuation, incorrect spelling and other variations of English usage render an otherwise promising manuscript virtually worthless. The researcher should give importance more to clarity than style.
- One should take care of the economy of words and concentration of ideas and brevity. Repetition and superfluousness will obstruct the lucidity of the report.
- One should write an unbiased, objective report fortified by facts.
- Colloquial or conversational mode of writing is inappropriate in a research report A thesis should not consist of the reporting of personal experience or opinion but should be critical analysis of the problem
- Readability is another aspect which a researcher should bear in mind. Sentences should not be too complex nor crammed with jargon
- The report should focus on the target audience.

## Drafting of the Report

The research report should normally go through three drafts. The objective of the first draft is comprehensiveness and fullness of facts. In the second draft the report should be improved both in the form and the language by considerable trimming and pruning ideas and sentences have to be realigned so that the report gets clarity, order, logic, unity, coherence and naturalness. Presentation of research data in the form of charts, tables graphs, figures enables not only to present the data in a readable form but also helps the reader to understand the more complex tabulations. The final draft should concentrate on the final touches on documentation to make the report authoritative and convincing. References and bibliography would make the citations more authoritative. For the preparation of citations style manuals may be followed. Citations should be consistent and complete in all respects.

## Fundamentals of style and Grammar

A precise and clearly worded research report should be free from grammatical mistakes and must ensure that correct forms of verbs are used, capitalization is used for the first letters of proper names, place names and the first letters of all words in titles of publications excluding words that are articles or conjunctions. Title of books, films, plays and poems should be italicized. To promote unity and logical thought, sentences must not contain too many ideas. Simple sentence should be used rather than complex one.

## Organisation of Information in Research Report- Dissertation / Thesis

In respect of organisation of information, dissertation and thesis has more or less similar components. The information in the research report should be logically arranged in the following components or structure. The components include Preliminaries, the main body or the text of the report and auxiliaries in order.

## The preliminaries must include the following elements

- Title page should include title of the research topic, statement of submission –eg. 'Dissertation/Thesis submitted to University of Kerala in partial fulfillment of the requirements for the award of the degree Master of Library and Information Science/ Doctor of Philosophy in Library & Information Science', Name of the researcher, Name of the research centre, year of submission.
- Declaration – 'I hereby declare that the dissertation/thesis entitled ' Manpower utilisation in the special libraries in Kerala' is a bonafide record of research work carried out by me and that the dissertation/thesis has not previously

formed the basis for the award of any Degree or Diploma, Associateship, Fellowship or other similar title of any university'. Name and Signature of the candidate may be given in the declaration.

**Certificate of the Supervising Teacher :** Certificate may be in the form, 'Certified that the dissertation/thesis entitled,' Manpower utilisation in the special libraries in Kerala' submitted by Mr/Ms..................for the award of the Master of Library & Information Science/ Doctor of Philosophy in of University of Kerala is a record of bonafide research work done under my guidance and supervision and that it has not previously formed the basis for the award of any Degree, Diploma, Fellowship or Associateship.' Name of the Supervising Teacher.

**Acknowledgement :** This element of the dissertation/thesis a word of thanks to those who have helped the author in the conduct of the study.

**Table of contents :** This area consists of chapter number, name of the chapter, sub sections of the chapter and respective page numbers.

**Abstract :** It should be a distillation of the thesis, forms the concise description of the problem(s) addressed, method of solving it, results and conclusion.

**List of tables, List of figures, List of abbreviations :** This consists of list of tables, figures and abbreviation in the format, number, title and page number.

This abstract should be self-contained.

The body of the Report

The body of the report is organized under the following chapters

**Chapter 1. Introduction**

This chapter contains the following elements

- Relevance of the study
- Title, statement of the problem

- Objective of the study
- Hypothesis/ Hypotheses
- Scope and limitations of the study
- Significance of the study
- Organisation of the study

**Chapter 2. Review of related studies**

This chapter forms the review of previous studies related to the field of investigation.

**Chapter 3. Research Methodology/Methods**

This chapter contains detailed account of the research methodology and various types of methods adopted for the conduct of the study.

**Chapter 4. Background of the study**

In this chapter the background information relating to the topic under study should be provided.

**Chapter 5. Analysis and Discussion**

Analysis and interpretation of the data collected through, historical method, survey method, experimental method etc can be provided in this chapter

**Chapter 6. Findings and conclusion/Findings and Recommendation**

This chapter provides the major findings evolved out from the analysis and interpretation of data. It also contains recommendations or suggestions, suggested areas for further research, validation of the hypotheses and conclusions.

**Auxiliaries** : The auxiliaries include the following elements

- **Appendix/ Appendices** : This may be questionnaire schedule, interview schedule or any other long list of items not provided in the text.

- **Glossary** : Technical terms and their meaning used in the text
- **Bibliography./References** : Alphabetical list of sources consulted in the preparation of the dissertation /thesis is provided.

## 6.26. Organisation of Information in Project Proposal

A project proposal is one of the media of communication grouped under technical writing. It is considered as blueprint of a research work to be undertaken by a researcher. The success of a research work highly depends on how a project proposal is clearly and objectively delineated. Moreover, the acceptance of the project by the concerned authorities also depends on how judiciously and objectively the proposal is presented. Hence much attention should be bestowed by the investigator while preparing the project proposal. A research proposal may be prepared as part of an academic programme for Master's degree. M.Phil, Ph.D or D.Litt. There is another kind of research, which is carried out by researchers as part of scholarly pursuit, which is not for a degree. This type of research is usually conducted by researchers by utilizing the finance received from internal or external agencies. In the preparation of proposals for both academic and non-academic research programmes the components in the proposal have common features or elements in general. This chapter enumerates the agencies engaged in awarding research project, components of a research project, qualities of a good research project and an example of project proposal.

### Levels and Agencies of Research

A number of agencies are engaged in supporting research project by providing financial assistance to undertake projects. These agencies include international, national, state and local agencies. The organizations viz UNESCO, UNDP, FAO, WHO, ILO Ford Foundation etc are some of the international agencies engaged in promoting research by providing financial assistance for researches. In India national organizations viz. UGC, CSIR, ICSSR,

DST, ICHR, Ministry of Human Resources Development, Raja Ram Mohan Roy Library Foundation etc are some of the major organizations engaged in awarding research projects to researchers. At the state level Department of Science and Technology. Department of Education etc are agencies encouraging research activities. In addition to these agencies, Universities and R and D Organizations at the local level invite research proposals from prospective researchers. In the preparation of proposals for submission to any of the above agencies a number of factors should be considered. These include scope of the agency, thrust areas of research of each agency, guidelines given by each agency in the preparation of projects proposal etc. Most of the agencies have brought out guidelines for the preparation of project proposals. The researcher should follow all these guidelines while preparing the project proposal.

The format of the proposal to be submitted to some of the important funding agencies is detailed below.

The UGC guidelines for submission of project proposal comprise the following components.

(i) Objective of the study
(ii) Justification of the study
(iii) Relevance of an action programme
(iv) Approach and Methodology
(v) Details of data collection and analysis
(vi) Project duration
(vii) Staffing pattern, Budget, and
(viii) Institution's own contribution

The ICSSR has prescribed a format for the submission of research proposals, which should contain the following components.

(i) The title of the project
(ii) Statement of the problem
(iii) Overview of literature

(iv) The conceptual framework

(v) Research questions or Hypotheses

(vi) Converge

(vii) Data collection

(viii) Data processing

(ix) Time Budgeting

(x) Organisational Framework; and

(xi) Cost Estimation

The State Committee on Science, Technology and Environment, Government of Kerala has prescribed a format for the submission of proposals for funded research work. The proposal should contain the following components of information.

(i) Title of the research proposal

(ii) Broad areas of research

(iii) Project type (Basic Research/ Applied Research/ Developmental/ Demonstration/others)

(iv) Objectives of the project (150 characters)

(v) Applications/Socio-economic importance of the project

(vi) Abstract (300 characters)

(vii) Name of the investigator with bio-data

(viii) Particulars of manpower required

(ix) Particulars of equipments required

(x) Particulars of any other facilities required

(xi) Particulars of the facilities that will be provided by the institution where this project will be implemented, and

(xii) Budget details

## Elements or Components of a Research Proposal

The essential Elements or Components required for a typical research proposal to be submitted for research are the following.

(a) Title Page

(b) Abstract
(c) Table of Contents
(d) Introduction
(e) Review of related Studies
(f) Research Design
(g) Analysis of Data
(h) Institutional Infrastructure
(i) Manpower
(j) Budget
(k) Anticipated Results of the study
(l) Timetable
(m) References/Bibliography and Appendices

**Title Page**

The title of the research project should be short, clear, properly worded and self-explanatory. Lengthy and fanciful title should be avoided. The title page should also contain the name of the research scholar and the place and name of the institution to which the project work is affiliated.

**Abstract**

A research proposal should contain an informative abstract consisting of about 200-300 words. It should contain the important elements of the proposals such as relevance, objectives, methodology/ies, hypothesis, data analysis methods, limitations, if any, timetable etc. In the primary selection of a project proposal the abstract will help the expert in the selection procedures without reading the entire project proposal. Hence utmost care should be taken in the preparation of the abstract.

**Table of Contents**

The major elements of the project proposal should be brought under the table of contents. The various components of the proposal have to be linked with pagination, which will help the experts to verify any component in the proposal with ease.

## Introduction

The Purpose of this component is to introduce the topic to be investigated in all its dimensions. Relevance of the topic of research to be investigated should be emphasized. The general objectives and specific objectives should be clearly drawn. Definition of kernel terms in the title of the research should be given. The significance of the topic in the contemporary research may also be provided. In fact the researcher introduces the topic in such a way as to indicate that the topic selected is so important and worthy to be investigated.

## Review of Related Studies

As a background of the topic of research a survey of related studies should be given under this head. The objectives, methodology and important findings of the related studies can be provided. The review should be selective and organized in a systematic order. This component will help the researcher in getting a clear idea about the methodology/ies and findings in the similar studies or related studies conducted earlier. The review of related studies will also help the evaluator of the project proposal to understand that the study to be conducted is not a repetitive one but an original one.

## Research Design

Research Design constitutes methodology/ies, hypotheses, testing of hypothesis, Research approach, methods of gathering data, techniques of gathering data and data gathering instruments used in the study. Detailed description about methodology/ies to be adopted in the study should be provided. The methodologies adopted should be suitable to the problem to be studied. Hypothesis should be formulated objectively. The hypothesis should be clear, crisp, short and wise and should be verifiable. The researcher should spell out the research approaches such as historical research, survey research and experimental research and the categories under which the study is to be made. Methods of gathering data, techniques of gathering data and data gathering instruments etc. have to be adequately described in the project proposal. If the study adopts sampling techniques, adequate description of type of sample should be provided.

**Analysis of Data**

The researcher should describe the type of data analysis, which is proposed to be conducted in the proposed study. The data analysis to be conducted manually or by using computers should be described in the project proposal. In case any computer statistical package is intended to be used in the data analysis this has to be mentioned in the proposal.

**Institutional Infrastructure.**

The institutional infrastructure is another component, which supports the success of the research project. The institutional facilities such as library, laboratory, computers and space for accommodating project staff in the office etc should be provided.

**Manpower**

In the case of a major project, a number of personnel may be required. In such situation the number of persons required, qualifications of the staff, experience etc should be given in the project proposal.

**Budget**

A statement relating to the expenditure requirement for completing the project work may be given as financial memorandum. Financial memorandum has to be prepared for funded research project. The budget should be a realistic one. Separate statements should be prepared under recurring and non-recurring heads. A typical budget would comprise of the following items.

(i) Salary/Wages

(ii) Stationery and postage

(iii) Printing and Xeroxing charges

(iv) Books and Journals

(v) Rent of building, cost of furniture etc.

(vi) Equipments

(vii) Travelling Allowance

(viii) Computer data analysis charges

(ix) Miscellaneous expenses

(x) Overhead expenditure

**Anticipated results of the Study**

The details relating to the anticipated results from the study may be provided to show the significance of the study. These results may be considered by the funding agency for approving the proposal to conduct the study as a significant one.

**Limitations of the study**

Limitations, if any, in conducting the investigation by the researcher should be explained objectively. The limitation may be usually in respect of the specificity of the topic of investigation. This will help the researcher to pinpoint the research topic proposed to be undertaken.

**Time table**

The project should spell out the time required to complete the proposed project work. The investigator should also propose a timetable to execute various jobs associated with the project work. The break up of time can be considered for the various activities under the heads time required for background work, time required for data collection, time required for data analysis and time required for writing the research report. The timetable for executing various jobs in the proposal will enable the researcher to complete the research work in time.

### References/Bibliography and Appendices

References cited in the proposal may be organized at the end of the proposal. The documents consulted for the preparation of the report may also be grouped under bibliography. Appendix/es, if any should also be given at the end of the proposal.

### Qualities of a Good Proposal.

The project proposal as a technical document should have some essential characteristics or attributes and qualities. According to Krishan Kumar the following are some of the features of a good project proposal.

It should

(i) Have an attractive format, free from typographical errors,

(ii) Contain only that information which would enable understanding of the problem and its proposed solution.

(iii) Be precise, well written and easy to understand

(iv) Reflect imagination in research design

(v) Give evidence of clear thinking.

(vi) Show adequate grasp of research and statistical tools applicable to the study.

(vii) Represent a high level of scholarship, giving evidence of deep insight into the problem.

(viii) Be clearly and logically organized, and

(ix) Above all give enough evidence of the application of scientific method of inquiry

A research proposal should be prepared by the researcher with due care. A researcher should be capable of selecting an appropriate topic for the research. A researcher should also take care to structure *i.e.*; the proposal with various components of a research proposal in tune with the guidelines provided by the funding agencies. A research proposal, which is error free and is qualitatively a good one, will be approved for pursuing the research. ICSSR guidelines for the formulation of a research project proposal is given below..

Project directors are to furnish a detailed research proposal covering the statement of the problem, the principal research questions posed or the hypotheses to be tested, if any; the definition of key concepts, the research design including the universe of study, the sampling frame, and type of sampling procedure where applicable; tools to be used in data collection; time schedule; staffing pattern; and an estimate of costs. The proposal should invariably be accompanied with a forwarding letter (in the form prescribed) from the institution.

A research proposal is a sort of a blueprint. Apart from helping the ICSSR to process it quickly, a well-conceived research proposal will later also help in its efficient implementation. Every effort made to formulate a proper research proposal will, therefore, pay rich dividends. Social Science research is characterized by a diversity of theoretical perspectives, substantive orientation methodological strategy, data collection practice and analysis technique. It is, therefore, not possible to indicate in short space all the possible ways in which a research proposal can be framed. However, there are certain characteristics that are common to all research proposals. These characteristics are:

(a) formulation of a problem for research

(b) delimiting the boundary of the proposed research and elaboration of its substantive components.

(c) source and method of data collection; and

(d) data analysis

Given these similar characteristics, individual research proposals will vary greatly in the selection of a researchable problem and the delineation of subsequent steps necessary to complete the research. The selection of a researchable problem depends on the inclination, training and experience of the research scholar. Whatever the problem be one must take care to see that it is researchable-one.. Whether one is motivated by the former or the latter, will have important bearing on how the research proposal is developed and designed. The former objective requires a kind of mapping out operation of usually a segment of social reality in respect of certain of its characteristics supposed to be important. If, on the other hand, the purpose is to explain the occurrence of a particular social phenomenon, the emphasis is on why does that particular phenomenon occur and what factors explain its occurrence either in causal or associational terms. It is obvious, then, that these two types of researches require entirely different strategies.

Whatever be the purpose of research, it is apparent that the selection of essential characteristics for either mapping out a particular aspect of social reality or for explaining its occurrence requires the placing of the problem and its dimensions in some context. The context must be provided by the accumulated social science knowledge on the one hand, and the theoretical position one takes in regard to the problem at hand, on the other. As such, a proper research design must start out with formulating a researchable problem and proceed on to locate it in some theoretical perspective and link it up with whatever social science findings exist in the area of enquiry. An overview of pertinent literature in the area of enquiry, therefore, becomes a crucial component of a research design. The purpose of the overview of literature is not to list the number of published, either all or a few well-known works but to cull out important findings that relate to the substantive concern of the proposed research. This culling out of important finding is necessary for determining the salience of the problem itself. On the one hand, it illuminates the theoretical perspective one brings to bear on the problem of research, on the other, thereby it helps in the cumulating of social science knowledge.

That there is an intimate relationship between the delineation of theoretical perspective and the overview of literature needs no demonstration. Theoretical perspective informs the overview of literature in terms of selection of scholarly works and of findings in order to illustrate their relevance or insufficiency for the enquiry into the problem at hand. Whether the delineation of theoretical perspective proceeds or follows the overview of literature is a matter of individual preference. However, what must be emphasized here is the necessity of linking up in some meaningful way of the overview of literature and the delineation of theoretical perspective. This is most important since it provides the backdrop for choosing the dimensions that must be explored for a particular enquiry.

Whether it is a descriptive or an explanatory research design, the problem taken up for investigation is invariably rooted in a complex and multifaceted social reality. It is, therefore, necessary to indicate aspects of social reality most relevant for that particular problem. The determination of the appropriate aspects takes its character from the theoretical perspective one adopts. This also describes the boundary of research and provides a basis for ascertaining the nature of data required for the conduct of enquiry.

Usually the determination of the dimensions of a research enterprise is expressed in the language of concepts relating to particular domains of social reality. Since it is a concept or a domain that conjoins theoretical knowledge with empirical reality, it is very important to clearly and precisely define the various concepts or domains proposed to be used in a research project. Also, since a concept or a domain represents an abstraction, the empirical references that constitute that abstraction must be specified. In other words, the concepts and domains have to be operationalized so that the passage between concepts and their empirical referents is made easy and scientifically valid.

While a descriptive research design need not go beyond the delineation of dimensions and their operationalization, explanatory research design must provide additional information on how the explanatory exercise is to be carried out. It should, first, indicate clearly the factors with the help of which one proposes to explain a particular phenomenon and second, enumerate hypothesized relationship among variables. In other words, the proposal must furnish an explanatory model containing variables linked with one another by some kind of interaction supposed to be taking place among them. Thus, the determination of independent and dependent variables and formulation of appropriate hypotheses are the essential characteristics of an explanatory research design.

The next step in a research design consists of the specification of the type of data to be collected, the manner in which they are to be collected and the unit to which they pertain. The data to be collected may, depending upon the nature of problem under investigation, be found almost 'ready-made' in various types of secondary sources or it may have to be generated. In the former case, the sources or required data must be indicated. In the case of the latter, construction of some kind of instrument-questionnaire, schedule, etc, for data gathering becomes necessary. In certain cases data have to be collected through interview, observation or the use of informants. In any case the manner in which data are to be collected must be specified. Also, the unit-individual, aggregate or some other entity about which data are to be collected-should also be indicated. In many cases it is just not possible to cover all the cases of a particular phenomenon even though it may seem desirable. The constraints of time and resources impose the necessity of selecting a few cases that may be deemed to be representing the entire class. Sampling then becomes an essential part of certain kinds of research design. When sampling is an integral part of a research design, the sampling frame, sampling procedure and sample size must be clearly elaborated and an adequate justification provided for the choice. In certain other cases, especially in respect of case studies or exploratory studies, when the focus of study is just one unit, detailed justification for a particular unit must find a place in the proposal.

When requisite data have finally been gathered, the data must be recorded in such a fashion that data processing according to some analysis plan becomes easy. It should be pointed out that data collected for particular purposes do not exhaust their possibilities when that purpose is served. The data can fruitfully be used by other scholars for secondary analysis, as such recording of data must provide for the possibility of reuse by others. This is especially true of quantifiable or quantified data which when recorded in a machine-readable form, lend themselves easily to re-analysis. It is, therefore, desirable to put these data in machine-readable form. The proposal should also provide for this and indicate the lines on which data are proposed to be analysed. Specially in the case of an explanatory research design, the analysis plan indicating coding design, the procedure of construction of indices and scales, the use of various statistical techniques for testing the direction and strength of hypothesized relationships, etc. must be included in the research design.

The above discussion suggests that a proper research design should be framed on the basis of the following guidelines, which are only illustrative.

### I. The Title of the project

### II. Statement of the Problem

In the opening paragraphs of the research proposal, the problem to be investigated should be stated clearly and briefly. The key questions and the location of the problem in the theoretical context of the concerned discipline should be specified. The significance of the problem, the contribution, which the proposed study is expected to make, theory and methodology as well as its practical importance and national relevance should be specifically indicated.

### III. Overview of Literature

Summarizing the current status of research in the area, including major findings, the project proposal should clearly demonstrate the relevance of insufficiency of the findings or approaches for the investigation of the problem at hand.

### IV. The Conceptual Framework

Given the problem and the theoretical perspective for investigating the problem, the proposal should clearly indicate the concepts to be used and demonstrate their relevance for the study. It should further specify the dimensions of empirical reality that need to be explored for investigating the problem.

### V. Research Questions or Hypotheses

Given the conceptual framework and the specification of dimensions, the specific questions to be answered through the proposed research should be sharply formulated.

In the case of an explanatory research design, specification of variables and posting of relationship among them through specific hypotheses must form a part of the research proposal.

### VI. Coverage

If in the light of the questions raised or the hypotheses proposed to be tested, sampling becomes necessary, full information on the following points should be given.

1. Universe of study
2. Sampling frame
3. Sampling procedure
4. Units of observation and sampling size.

If the study requires any control groups, these should be specifically mentioned. An explanation of the determination of size and type of sample will also be necessary. Proposals not requiring a sample selection should specify their strategy appropriately and describe the rationale.

### VII. Data Collection

The different types of data that are proposed to be gathered should be specifically mentioned.

The sources for each type of data and the tools and techniques that will be used for collecting different types of data should be specified.

For questionnaire or schedule to be used, the following should be indicated.

1. Distribution of questionnaire or schedule in different sections, eg. identification data, socio-economic data, questions on various sub-themes.
2. Approximate number of questions to be asked each respondent.
3. Any scaling techniques to be included in the instrument
4. Any projective tests incorporated to the questionnaire/ schedule.
5. Approximate time needed per interview.
6. Any plans for index-construction.
7. Coding plan (whether the questions and responses will be pre-coded or not, whether the coding is don e for computer, or for hand tabulation)

For interviews, the following details should be given.

1. How they are to be conducted (free associational, non-directive, focused, direct or on telephone).
2. Particular characteristics that interviews must have for the use of observation techniques, described.
3. The type of observation: quasi-participant, non-participant,
4. Units of observation;
5. Whether this will be the only technique or whether other techniques will also be employed.

**VIII. Data Processing**

The manner in which the different types of data will be processed, the tabulation plan and the types of data that will be processed through the computer should be explained in detail.

### IX. Time Budgeting

The project should be broken up in suitable stages and the time required for the completion of each stage of work should be specified. For instance, such stages may cover.

1. Preparatory work, including selection and appointment of staff and their training.
2. Pilot study, if any.
3. Drawing of sample.
4. Tool construction (including their pre testing and printing).
5. Data collection.
6. Data processing (which should include coding, editing, sorting, computer analysis).
7. Data analysis
8. Report writing.

### X. Organizational Framework

An organizational chart indicating the position, tasks, and number of persons, their level of qualifications/training required to fill the different positions should be given.

### XI. Cost Estimation

The cost of the project is to be estimated in terms of total man-months and the facilities needed. Calculate it under the following headings.

| (1) Personnel Position | No. of Person | Salary (Including Allowances, etc.) | Duration | Amount Required |
|---|---|---|---|---|
| (1) | (2) | (3) | (4) | (5) |

2. Travel
3. Data processing
4. Stationery and printing

5. Equipment (total expenditure not to exceed 5 per cent of the total budget)
6. Books, journals, etc. (expenditure not to exceed 5 per cent of the total)
7. Contingency expenses including postage
8. Any other (specify)
9. Overhead charges 5 per cent of the cost (i.e., of the sum of items 1 through 8, where Applicable)
10. Grand total

While suggesting budget estimates for the research proposal the project director should take into account the time, budget, as well as various steps involved in the conduct of the research proposal.

The rationale for the allocation of time and money for the various items of budget estimates must be furnished.

A model of a project proposal is given below for potential researchers for the preparation of research project.

# In Formation Technology Awareness Programme For College Students in Kerala- A Proposal (Project Proposal Submitted to the Ministry of Information Technology, Government of India)

*Project Director*

DR. G. DEVARAJAN

*Head, Department of Library and Information Science*

Project Affiliated: Department Of Library Information Science, University Of Kerala, Trivandrum-34.

## ABSTRACT

Discusses the avenues of information technology in the qualitative improvement of present day education. Emphasises the role of information technology in the effective learning process of students in higher education. Formulates the general and specific objectives of the study. Describes the type of population studied and methodologies followed for the conduct of the study. Discusses the methods and media to be used for the Information Technology awareness programme among students. These include lecture method, and audio-visual methods. Data analysis methods, period of execution of the project, institutional resources and project affiliation, manpower etc. are provided, Detailed budget estimates under non-recurring and recurring heads for a total amount of Rs.29, 85,000/- are proposed for the conduct of the project work.

## TABLE OF CONTENTS

## Introduction

The societal development of a nation is highly dependent on the type and quality of education imparted at the various levels. Since education is a specific mode of social practice and collective endeavour made by the society in a particular set of environments, neither its meaning not its form can remain the same for a long time. And when the conditions of our social existence undergo a change, significant shifts in the content and form of education are imperative. A radical transformation in education especially in higher education is called for. In order to bring out such a change the avenues in information technology can be fruitfully utilized in education. The avenues of information technology in disseminating information from the generator to the recipient at a faster rate have high relevance in the qualitative improvement of present day education.

Information technology can play a crucial role in the effective learning process of students engaged in higher education. Today a lot of information is generated through printed media and mass media which has resulted in the phenomenon, "information explosion" or "information flood". This will make the students of higher education meet with a number of problems in making use of available literature in their field of study comprehensively, speedily and with precision. But today because of the progress in information technology a student of higher education can make use of Multimedia, CD-ROM databases, on-line data bases,. INTERNET sources etc. for a voyage from sources that are available in any part of the globe in his/her field of study. But, are they aware of and capable of using the information technology tools to navigate in the sea of information? Are they proficient in navigating subject gateways and Internet tracking? There is lack of awareness to make use of these information technology gadgets especially among students who are studying in the colleges situated in the rural areas. This will lead to underutilization of the information resources, even if I.T. tools are made available in colleges. Hence it is imperative to conduct information technology awareness programmes among college students in the rural sectors to equip them to make use of these tools and resources effectively. It is hoped that this will enable them to overcome quite a lot of problems in learning process confronted by the rural student community when compared to the students in urban areas and also will ensure qualitative learning and quality education in the information age.

The main objective of the programme is to provide awareness programmes in information technology resources and tools to students in colleges especially in rural areas. More specifically the aim of the programme is:

(i) to provide basic information about computer and its peripherals;

(ii) to introduce various electronic information sources;

(iii) to impart programmes in multimedia information search;

(iv) to introduce students to CD-ROM in various subjects and how to search for these sources, Internet tracking, proficiency in navigating subject gateways; and

(v) to introduce students about IN TERNET sources and impart training in INTERNET and on-line information search programmes.

## Review of Literature

In a study Wood and others report that undergraduate students use computer-based information retrieval services in relation to their cognitive and learning styles. Includes a survey of staff at Sheffield University, UK on their use of computer databases and the extent to which undergraduates are made aware of these services. Results show that only a low percentage of undergraduates use them and there is great variation among students of different faculties. It also shows that, computer assisted learning packages were developed and customized for three departments (1). Charlotte and others in a study point out that the children, mainly 9-14 years old boys use the computer games.

The study also points out that quality game and educational programmes are available for use by children (2) Janet Abernethy in a study asserts that as the technological revolution sweeps the country, it is increasingly vital that children become computer literate. Public library has a vital role to play in introducing this technology through the provision of equipment, programmes and elementary instruction to users (3). Wrong in a study traces the development of the national information technology programme for education in Singapore. The study outlines the various developmental stages that cover initiation (before 1990), consolidation (1990-95) and leapfrogging after 1995 where topics like Internet, multimedia, networking, virtual reality and information superhighways are focused upon (4).

**The Research Design**

The Information Technology awareness programme will be confined to college students in Kerala. About 300 colleges affiliated to seven universities are working in Kerala. Of these, about 50% of colleges are located in rural areas. The students in these colleges are the target population of this programme. The awareness programme will be conducted for Degree, post-Graduates and research students. I.T. awareness programmes that are suitable to each level of student community will be conducted separately.

The following methods and media will be used for the programmes

(i) Lecture method

(ii) Audio-visual methods

(iii) Computer assisted teaching

(iv) Distribution of course materials

The above methods/s and media will be used for the programme depending upon the level of students community.

**Institutional Infrastructure**

The institutional infrastructure available in the Department of Library and Information Science, University of Kerala will be utilized for the successful conduct of the project. This project will also be affiliated to the Department of Library and Information Science, University of Kerala.

## Manpower

The manpower required for the execution of the project includes one Director, one programme Officer, one Audio-visual Operator and one Driver.

## Budget

| **Non-Recurring Expenditure** | | |
|---|---|---|
| Computer (Pentium III) 64 MB RAM (With multimedia kit) | One | Rs.1,00,000.00 |
| Laser printer | - One | Rs. 40,000.00 |
| LCD projector (Colour) | - One | Rs. 3,50,000.00 |
| OHP (portable type) | - One | Rs. 30,000.00 |
| CD-ROMS, Floppy disks etc. | - | Rs. 25,000.00 |
| Software packages | - | Rs. 2,50,000.00 |
| Vehicle (Omni Van) | - One | Rs. 2,50,000.00 |
| Printing, Stationary and postage | - | Rs. 50,000.00 |
| Overhead expenditure | - | Rs. 50,000.00 |
| **Total Non-recurring expenditure Rs. 11,45,000.00** | | |

| **Recurring Expenditure** | |
|---|---|
| Project Director (one)@Rs.15,00pm (1500x12x5) - (Honorarium) | Rs. 90,000.00 |
| Programme Officer (One)@Rs.5,000pm (5000x12x5) (Salary) | Rs.1,80,000.00 |
| Audio-visual operator (One)@Rs.3,000pm (3000x12x5) (Salary) | Rs.1,50,000.00 |
| Petrol and other maintenance to vehicle | Rs.1,00,000.00 |
| AMC to PC INTERNET connectivity, repairs of Equipments etc. | Rs. 50,000.00 |
| Vehicle tax | Rs. 20,000.00 |
| Overhead expenditure | Rs. 50,000.00 |

| | |
|---|---|
| **Total Recurring expenditure** | **Rs.9,40,000.00** |
| **Grand total (Non-recurring and Non-recurring expenditure)** | **Rs.29,85000.00** |

## ANTICIPATED RESULTS OF THE STUDY

The project will enable to create an information technology awareness among student community in Kerala. This in turn will help the student community to solve a number of problems confronted by them in the field of education.

## TIME TABLE

The duration of the project will be five years from the academic year 2001 June to 2006 June. The period of the project can be extended, after evaluation of the five years programme as the second phase of the project.

## 6.27. ORGANISATION OF INFORMATION IN HOUSE JOURNAL

House journal is an important tool for communication among members or employees of an institution or leaned body or company. It is known in various names such as House organ, in-house Magazine, in-house publication, shop paper, plant paper, employees Magazine, News letter, News Bulletin etc. It can be defined as a serial consisting of a few pages, usually printed, containing new born information or news which is of interest to a special or particular group of users. It is usually produced by large organisations as a medium of dissemination of news and activities for the benefit of its employees and has a limited circulation. The organisations which publish house journal may be international bodies, national bodies, individual institutes, companies, associations or societies.

The genesis of house journal goes back to Chinese Han Dynasty which used this type of communications to keep the court informed. This is considered as the forerunners of today's journals. An early publication, 'Travellers Record' by Travellers Insurance Company was started in 1865. This publication is now called

'Projections'. The first house journal from India is 'Planters Chronicle which was published by the United Planters Association of South India during 1905.

**Types of House Journal.**

The house journals can be classified into

- Technical journal
- Magazine – News letters
- Periodical catalogue -similar to trade literature

On the basis of the users of house journals these can be categorised into :

External publications that are intended for external audience and internal publication that are intended for internal audience.

**Characteristics of House Journal**

House journal is a periodical publication which is published with a periodicity usually semi-monthly, monthly, bimonthly etc. An issue consists of 4,8,16 or 24 pages and in some may be 40 pages. It contains different types of columns, each for a news story, feature story, personality story, background story, capsule story etc.

**Functions of House journal**

The basic aim of any house bulletin/ newsletter is to stimulate intellectual curiosity of the public in the activities /events of an organisation and to encourage participation. Other functions are : i) It is a type of publicity material which aims at announcing in a capsule form information about current events, activities, publications, research studies, products, designs, employment news etc of relevance to the users concerned. ii) It publishes timely and relevant activities of current interest. Iii) It informs users, especially academic and research staff, about forthcoming conferences, seminars, symposia, meetings etc to facilitate their participation. iv) It also serves as a medium for reporting and communicating information about social and cultural activities, personnel information, appointments, transfers, retirements, marriage, obituary etc. in the organisation.

### Preparation of House Journal

The steps involved in the preparation of House journal conforms, generally, to the methodology for the preparation of information consolidation products. These include the following

- Identification of users and their informational requirements
- Scope definition
- Collection of information
- Appraisal of information collected for inclusion in the house journal
- Presentation of information including textual and non-textual presentations
- Finalisation –involving checking and editing
- Physical production of house journal.

### Content Organisation in House journal

The contents of a house journal /News letter generally constitutes the following items of information relating to an organisation,

(i) A regular feature entitled from the Chairman's desk, Director's desk

(ii) A short editorial

(iii) A topical feature

(iv) A regular feature on a specific topic

(v) The welfare activities

(vi) Humour pages

(vii) A regular feature of cultural events/activities

## 6.28. SCRIPTS FOR AUDIO-VISUAL PRESENTATION

The term audio-visual may refer to works with a sound

and a visual component, the production or use of such works, or to equipment used to create and present such works. Slide tape presentation, films and television programme are examples of audio-visual presentations. Once audio-visual media came into existence, it became a part of people's everyday lives within a few decades.

In a typical presentation, the presenter provides the audio by speaking and supplements it with a series of images projected onto a screen, either from a slide projector, or from a computer connected to a projector using presentation programme.

In the developed world, there has been a huge uptake of computer-based audio-visual equipment in the education sector, with many schools and higher educational establishments installing projection equipment and often using interactive whiteboard technology.

A standard form of audio-visual presentation is a series of slides in a revolving projector, wherein the slides are synchronised with the sound track on a tape recorder. The slides are changed by a pulse recorded over the voice commentary on the tape. The technical writer's job is to write the supporting strip using a predetermined slide series. In this case, a simple brief on the nature of the subject may be enough to complete the writing of the script. For the audio-visual presentation, a person with a pleasant voice may be chosen to record the script. The entire approach in the production of the audio-visual presentation should be in the same way as any other writing task.

## General Rules for preparing Audio-visual materials

When preparing your audio-visual material, keep the time limit for your presentation in mind. 15 to 20 slides should be prepared for 25 minutes regular presentation. All slides must use landscape format. Colour should be used carefully and colour combination resulting in a low contrast should be avoided. The first slide should contain the title of your paper and the author names, your affiliations and your company or university logo. This will be the only page where a logo is permitted. You should also prepare the slides such as : a slide describing the motivation and the basic idea of your work; a slide containing an outline of your talk; and a slide containing the conclusion of your talk. Please make sure that index expressions are also readable. Please note that minimum font size requirements apply also to index expressions. Keep the material simple and uncluttered. Programme listings and very long equations should be avoided. Tables should be represented graphically, wherever possible. Do not use the valuable space on your slides for large company logos and other elements that do not help in motivation or understanding your work. Duplicates of slides should be produced in case the same information is needed twice.

Evans in his study Beginner's Guide to Technical writing' suggested the following tips in the preparation of scripts for audio-visual presentations.

- The material should be fully understandable and written to the level of expertise of the audience.
- A general overview should be followed by a progressive break down into relevant facts and details
- For conceptual material, abstract ideas may be illustrated by anecdotes or concrete examples.
- The audio-visual scripts are by nature highly concentrated and equally, highly selective in terms of detailed material.
- The length, a reasonable rule thumb, is about 2000 words can be spoken in 15 minutes.

## 6.29. CONTENT ORGANISATION IN WEBSITES

The website forms an important information source of any institution for imparting information about its services and products. The backbone of any website is its content. Web content is the recorded human communications. It is the textual, visual or aural content that is encountered as part of the user experience on websites. It may include, text, images, sounds, videos and animations. The content of the website may include documents, data, applications, e-services, images, audio and video files, personal web pages, archived e-mail messages etc.

Writing and preparing content for web requires a different approach from writing and preparing content for print documents and publications. In addition, writing content for the web that grabs attention and gets the results one wants requires special skills and attention.

In the web page design the following guidelines may be considered.

- Follow a simple and consistent design. Complex designs can confuse people, so keep it simple. A consistent design will let your readers concentrate on content.
- Do not create gratuitous graphics. Graphics are one reason for the interest in the web by both publishers and readers and should definitely be included in your web page if possible. Still, it is important not to overuse them. Blinking text and other excessive decorations can be distracting. Background colours and textures can affect download time. Think carefully about the colours and textures you choose for background s and the effects they will have on the readability of text.
- Give people cross links. Visitors should be able to move from one major page to another on your site without having to go back to your home page. Put cross links to all your major pages at the bottom of all major pages.
- Be careful about 'over linking'. While linking to the work of others in your organisation and throughout the world can help your readers, it can also lead to information overload.. It is important to balance linking within your page design. Too many links can be visual eyesore on the page and a distraction from the original information you want your readers to concentrate on.

- Do not create dead end links. Readers can get discouraged from returning to your pages when those pages are filled with empty links.
- Sign all pages. Place a standard signature at the bottom of all major pages. This signature should contain the name of the page owner, date of last update, organisation and an e-mail address for comments and reporting broken links.

**Elements of web content**

Today, millions of websites are available and millions of sites are being uploaded in the web world every year. Because of the intense competition and limited supply of reader attention, a majority of these new sites will fail. So the essentials of contemporary web content style and structure will give the content a much better chance of getting noticed and read. The following can be considered some of the parameters for quality web content.

**Visual design :** A website must be visually pleasing. Every top website needs an incredible visual design

**Headline and strong hook :** The headline is a key which creates a sense of interest and value. The hook is the interesting angle of the story that reaches out and snags people's attention – pulling them into reading the copy.

**User Interface :** The user interface is the foundation of any good functional web site. While designing a site, we should take into consideration the information need of the target audience

**Headers and Bulleted/ Numbered Lists :** Most users prefer to quickly scan web content diagonally, rather than actually read it. Having bold, nicely CSS(Cascading style sheet) sub headers make the content easier to look at and less intimidating to zip through in a hurry. Lists help people soak in important facts that would otherwise sail right user their radar.

**Primary Navigation :** An easy to navigate web site is ensuring that the primary means of navigation – links to the key areas of the site – are kept above the fold. Elements to include here are the logo as well as links to the main sections of the site.

**Navigation in the Footer :** It is especially important to offer a duplicate set of navigation links in the footer. Even if we use text links at the top, the duplication is still helpful. Some times the footer will link to additional information such as Terms of Service.

**Meaningful Content :** If the content is not informative and good, then the users are not going to stick around. So in the content development it is important to provide helpful, knowledgeable information about the institution, company, products and services etc.

**Quality Writing :** Quality writing is important. If the writing is murky, verbose or filled with errors, the content would not get shared and communicated.

**Photos and Illustrations :** Too much plain text is downright intimidating. Having one or more images in the text will make the content on the reader's eyes and brain.

**Separate Design from Content :** Nowadays html tables are not much used for layout and design. The best developed sites use a combination of XHTML and CSS (Cascading Style Sheets) which create a separation of design versus content.

**Contact Information :** Ideally there are more than one method of contact. E-mail address, contact form and phone number etc can be included in the site.

**Search :** A search field is incredibly helpful in any type of website. There is nothing like wading through hundreds of pages to find specific content without a search future. If a potential customer cannot find something easily on the site, the purpose of the website will not be satisfied. There should be functional search box attached with the site.

**Site Map :** A site map meant for visitors can be an invaluable tool for finding just what they are looking for. Creating a site map – a structural list of all pages of a website is especially useful if a search feature is not attached to the site. A link to the site map is another item that is helpful to place down in the footer of the site.

**Links to Sources and additional Information :** High-quality web content has text with hyperlinks to sources, proof and additional resources. This takes the content to a higher level of credibility.

## Web Content Development

Web content development is the process of researching, writing, gathering, organising and editing information for publication on websites. Website content may consist of prose, graphics, pictures, recording, movies or digital assets that could be distributed by hypertext transfer protocol server, and viewed by a web browser. The type of content one produces influences the popularity and profitability of your website. The contents need to be interactive and educational if one is operating a paid membership website. Also, content goes a long way in establishing the value of your website. Hence, having the right content development strategy can make a big difference in how fast your website grows.

As an illustrative example the content of a webpage of a university consists of the following elements of information as main heads and subheads.

- **General Information**

  Name and Address

  Year of Establishment

  History and Development

- **Administrative and Academic Bodies**

  Chancellor

  Pro-Chancellor

  Vice-Chancellor

  Pro-Vice-Chancellor

  Registrar

Controller of Examinations

Syndicate

Senate

Faculty

Board of Studies

- **Teaching and Research Departments**

Academic Departments

Faculty Information

Supporting Departments

Library

Academic Staff College

Publication Division

- **Courses Offered**

List of various courses/programmes

Schemes and Syllabus

- **Admission, Examination**

Registration of courses offered

Admission/Exam notification

Online Registration

Hall ticket

Time table

Examination Fee

Results

- **Affiliated Colleges**

Address of colleges/Institutions

Courses/programmes offered

Faculty Information

Website Accessibility

Seminars/Lectures Information

- **Student's Activities**

  Student's Union/ University Union

  Alumni

  National Service Scheme

  NCC
- **Facilities Provided**

  Search Option

  Feedback

  Print options

  E-mail/ web mail

  Download
- **Supporting Information**

  Sitemap

  Right to Information Act

  University Act/Statutes

  Photo Gallery

  FAQ

  Digital Archive
- **Value Added Information**

  Link to UGC/AICTE/Other Universities

  Link to E-Resources

  Placement Portal

  Blood Donors Directory

  Web Casting

The following are some guidelines or strategies for the content development.

**Content needs to capture attention** : Users prefer to read short articles. If you want many readers, focus on short and scannable content. If the users who really need solution,, focus on comprehensive coverage.

**Content Development should not be separated from strategic planning :** The content should be considered as part of your overall master plan and not just an isolated necessity or discipline. For generating revenue by volume in search engine traffic, sacrificing quality for quantity is not desirable. The strategy for content development that makes you an expert. As a different approach, content should demonstrate your knowledge and skills to be adopted.

**Content Differentiation :** Content differentiation helps you to survive and succeed in a crowded space. Content is only as good as the degree to which the users find it useful or entertaining. Subjectivity of content consumption is one of the main reasons why content dissemination and distribution channels are sometimes more important than the actual content quality.

The content of a web site is the substance that draws and keeps an audience. The composition of your content should follow directly from your stated web site purpose and audience. Currently the web content is no longer restricted to text, but has expanded to engulf other audio visual media. This includes video clips, presentations and a host of other interactive forms which can be picked up by the search engines

## REFERENCES

Abenethy, Janet: Computer literacy and children Canadian Library Journal 41(1) 1984 P. 26-29.

Abrahams, Mark A : Simple steps to writing an article. http://enzinearticles.com/article 49173.html

Charlotte, et al: Children gather in the computer workshop Bibliotek. 70(17) 1988 P. 640-41.

Evans, J(1993)Beginner's Guide to technical writing. Butterworth & Co, Indian Council of Social Science Research. (1999)ICSSR research grants. New Delhi, ICSSR,.

Kelly,Ivan: Easy steps to writing articles. http://www.populararticles.com/article49173.html

Kerala, Science and Technology, Dept(1995). Rules for the administration of the research fund, Kerala, Trivandrum, The Govt.

Krishan Kumar(1992). Research Methods in Library and Information Science, New Delhi, Vikas.

Russel, Nakand (2002) Web content management. Boston, Addison –Wesly.

White, JA, et al. Accessing ICLAS network log data to study student computer usage, course performance and attitude change. Journal of Information Technology for Teacher Education 3. (1) 1994 P. 79-89.

Wood, F, et al. Information skills for student centered learning a computer assisted learning approach. British Library research and Innovation Report (37) 1997 P 1-60.

# 7
# Information Consolidation and Repackaging

## 7.1. INTRODUCTION

Information consolidation is a technique used for packing and repackaging of information that would facilitate easy reading, understanding and thereby utilisation of information contained in the technical documents. It is not a universal remedy to information needs and problems, but it is one of the important approaches to be considered together with other important products and services. The information environment today demand quite a good number of value added services in the form of information consolidated products such as Review articles, Status reports or State- of-the -art reports, Trend reports, Information digests, Handbooks etc Hence it is imperative that Information managers should be equipped with the techniques, methodology and writing skills for the generation of effective information consolidated products and services.

## 7.2. INFORMATION CONSOLIDATION

The symposium on 'Information Analysis and

Consolidation' sponsored by UNESCO at Colombo, Sri Lanka in 1978 adopted the following definition.

'Information consolidation activity is used to define the responsibilities exercised by individuals, departments or organisation for evaluating and compressing relevant documents in order to provide definite user groups with reliable and concise new bodies of knowledge. Individuals or groups of individuals performing information consolidation activities would each constitute an information consolidation unit'

Saracevic and Wood (1981) have defined information consolidation elaborately that ' consolidated information is public knowledge, specifically selected, analysed, evaluated, and possibly restructured and repackaged for the purpose of serving some of the immediate decisions, problems and information needs of a defined clientele or social group, who otherwise may not be able to effectively and efficiently access and use this knowledge as available in the great amounts of documents or in its original form. The criteria for selection, evaluation, restructuring and repackaging of this knowledge are derived from the potential clientele. To be precise ' consolidated information is a text(s) or message(s) purposefully structured from existing public knowledge to affect the private knowledge and decisions of individuals who otherwise may not be able to effectively and efficiently access or use this public knowledge from the original documents or in the original structure and form'.

Information consolidation is a process of higher complexity than indexing and abstracting. However, offsetting the problem of higher complexity and need for greater resources is the higher value of consolidated information. On a general level information consolidation is justified for its contribution to the processes of socio- economic development. On a specific level its benefits can be argued as a contribution to problem solving and decision making.

## 7.3. PACKAGING AND REPACKAGING

Packaging of information is a physical recording, arrangement and presentation of information on a given medium and in a given form. While repackaging of information is rearrangement of physical media and /or forms in which information has been presented in a given medium and form of restructured information, which is tailored to the requirements of a specific clientele. In fact, repackaging of information refers to the presentation of information in more understandable, readable, acceptable and usable form. The main objective of repackaging is to enhance the acceptance and use of information products and the assimilation and recall of their contents. Saracevic and wood have stated that the repackaged information products will serve the following functions.

- as a time saving tool
- as a selective and systematic sorter of useful information
- as a means for more extensive information transmission and delivery
- as a translation tool
- as an opportunity for the practical application of research results
- as a means for the prompt delivery of relevant information.

## 7.4. OBJECTIVES

Lack of appropriate information is a problem confronted by the user population. Appropriate information connotes 'the right information at the right time in the right amounts and at the right comprehension level of a given group of users '. Available and accessible information is often unused because it is simply not presented in a content and form that are appropriate for a given group of users. Consolidation of information is suggested as a solution of problems caused by lack of appropriate information. As such, consolidated information or repackaged information is particularly geared toward increasing utilisation of information by various user groups. Information consolidation is a task which in itself requires considerable skills, efforts and resources. Efforts and resources are needed to establish and maintain information consolidation units, to ensure the essential cooperation between subject experts and information specialists and to educate and train professionals skilful in creating information consolidation products and associated services.

Saracevic and Wood bring out the following major objectives of information consolidation and information repackaging:

(i) To increase the effectiveness of information transfer to and within developing countries;

(ii) To encourage more intensive information use in a wide array of developmental activities; and

(iii) To widen the circle of the population of potential users particularly by fulfilling specific information needs for evaluated and synthesised information.

## 7.5. VALUE OF CONSOLIDATED INFORMATION

On a general level, information consolidation is justified for its contribution to the processes of social and economic development. On a specific level its benefits can be argued as a contribution to problem solving and decision making. The process of development in an increasingly interdependent world involves and requires an increase in sophistication and use of scientific, technical, commercial and related information. The value of such information does not lie in its existence but in its acceptance and use. In fact, chances for acceptance and use of information are increased by its being more appropriate. Consolidated information aims at being more appropriate to the users, their needs, and levels, the capacities and time allotments given to information absorption and similar user-related factors.

Saracevic suggests that the value of consolidated information can be argued in relation to its role in decision making and problem solving. Making decisions and solving problems, even those encountered in everyday work, requires information. Moreover: i) as complexity of decisions or problems increases, the need for information intensifies; ii) as the amount of available information proliferates, it becomes harder to get and use relevant information; iii)as complexity, interdisciplinary, and technical sophistication of available information increase, less can be used by decision makers and problem solvers as presented in its original form.

## 7.6. TARGET AUDIENCE

The target audience or user groups of consolidated information include a wide groups of professionals working in various organisations. These include Scientists, technologists, engineers, researchers working in the research and development(R & D) institutions in the field of manufacturing, health services, planning, education etc. User groups such as managers from industries, commerce and marketing are another strata of audience. Policy and decision makers in government, technicians, supervisors, paraprofessionals, communicators such as extension workers, agricultural and industrial workers etc are other target audience of various types of information consolidated products.

## 7.7. METHODOLOGY OF INFORMATION CONSOLIDATION AND REPACKAGING

The methodology of information consolidation encompasses a number of procedures or stages. These procedures can be passed through three planes of works or activities in idea plane, verbal plane and notational plane. The procedures of information consolidation in the conceptual level constitute idea plane, the procedures in the writing stages constitute verbal plane and the procedures relating to the grouping of ideas of main and sub-divisions by means of ordinal numbers constitute notational plane. The procedures involved in the information consolidation are:

- Initiation step
- Formulation of objectives and Identification of Target Group

- Scope determination
- Collection of information
- Evaluation of information collected
- Analysis and extraction
- Preparation of draft text
- Testing of draft
- Finalisation of the draft
- Dissemination of information
- Feedback from users

**(i) Initiation step**

The initiation step comprises two important activities viz ascertaining the need and demand of potential users and initiation of information consolidation work.

The key to the aims, direction and contents of any and all information consolidation activity is the users. There is much higher probability that products and services based on user studies will be better than those based on intuition, anecdotal, evidence or committee deliberations. The basic objective of a user study is to gather information that is useful in design, provision and evaluation of specific information consolidation products or services geared to specific users. In fact user studies are a necessity in all phases of information consolidation activities from design, to evaluation, to marketing, to management. So user study can be planned in order to ascertain the pertinent information needs or demands and preferential form of technical document required by the users in an institution. The user study plan includes: i) Surveying the previous studies and literature in general and learning about all aspects of user studies; ii) Determining the objectives of the study; iii) determining the variables to be studied; iv) selecting the sample ;v) determining the method of data collection ; vi) determine the method of data analysis; and vii) determining the ways of presentation and utilisation of results. The results of the study will give useful indices to information needs, types of information consolidated products required by users.

The initiation of information consolidated work also involves preparation of a panel of subject experts and information specialists for guidance and expert opinion in the course of various stages of information consolidation.

### (ii) Formulation of objectives and Identification of Target Group

In this stage the technical writer or the author has to decide the objective or purpose behind in bringing out the information consolidated product. Is the information product meant for introducing new ideas, or instructing or persuading or reporting findings? This would necessarily relate to identification of the target user group. In this context, information pertaining to the attributes of the user, such as specific purpose for which the user needs the information product, intellectual standard of the user, user's preferential form of information product etc can be collected.

### (iii) Scope Determination

In this stage, author has to determine the specific subject coverage and the type of technical document to be prepared. The subject scope involves the precise specification of a subject and would consist of recognising each of the component ideas and the correct degree of interrelation among them, and expressing the totality of the subject coextensively. For example in a subject of information consolidated product 'Cancer research in India during - 2005-10' the concepts such as cancer research, India, 2005-10, are to be taken into account coextensively to determine the specific subject of the technical document. The type of technical document involves the specification of the product to be prepared such as state-of-the art report, review article, critical review, information digest, handbook etc. This is usually determined on the basis of the purpose to which information is needed by the end users.

### (iv) Collection of Information

In this stage collection of document/information may be carried out based on the specific subject in mind as determined in the above stage. A comprehensive survey of the documentary sources such as primary, secondary, tertiary and non documentary sources such as formal and informal sources relevant in the field may be collected. This involves identification of specific information sources and selection of information sources. The information access tools and sources include : i) basic bibliographies; ii) selected lists of government and international organisations ; iii) reviews iv) reference books; v) content tables; vi) Indexing and abstracting sources and services; vii) SDI services viii) new titles information, publishers catalogues ix) human sources etc

The selection of information sources constitutes formulation or identification of criteria for selection and evaluation of information and information sources vis-a vis intrinsic value and user appropriateness.

### (v) Evaluation of information collected

Evaluation or appraisal is concerned with the determination of the intrinsic merit, validity, reliability and quality of information sources which will eventually be consolidated. There is often a consensus of what is information of higher quality, lesser quality, redundant, outdated or superseded information, inaccurate, wrong or false information. The consensus is built by applying certain criteria and tests as a yardstick against which the quality of information is judged.

Saracevic suggests that 'a single set of criteria for selection of sources for information consolidation to cover all kinds of products for all kinds of users cannot be justified. Different circumstances and objectives will clearly demand different criteria. However, guidance for development of specific selection and evaluation criteria can be derived from some of the generally recognised criteria used in: a) peer review and refereeing of publications in science and technology; and b) user evaluation of information products and services' Criteria in peer review and refereeing in publications in science and technology have long been used to judge meritorious work and reject work of little or no merit. These criteria are closely adaptable for selection of science and technology sources for information consolidation. These criteria are grouped under objective criteria and subjective criteria.

The objective criteria are:

- Underlying problems, facts, assumptions, parameters of thought: how well organised? Are assumptions warranted?
- Hypothesis, question, concepts: Are they clear and do they embody the problems, facts, parameters?
- Methods: are they appropriate, competent? Is there authoritative use of resources?
- Analysis: appropriate? Does it follow from facts collected?
- Interpretation: logical, common sense, strong?
- Validity : does the work stick to a defined problem, parameters, hypothesis?
- Reliability: accuracy, reflection of reality
- Awareness: Does it show a demonstration of knowledge of previous and related works.

The subjective criteria include: i) problem significance ;ii) solution significance; iii) Originality; iv) author institution; v) value vi) reporting style; and vii) publication.

The user evaluation of information services depends on users themselves and applies in judging the products and services received. The criteria include:

(i) Information or data quality: precision of information, credibility of the sources and recency of information

(ii) Scope: completeness of information, comprehensiveness of subject

(iii) Appropriateness: Fitting with needs; fitting with own capabilities

(iv) Haggle and hassle factors: time lag in receiving information; ease of usage; ease of access

(v) Costs :Direct and indirect costs for obtaining services.

**(vi) Analysis and Extraction**

This stage involves analysis and preparation of the informative abstract or extracts from the selected information sources/ information. The informative abstract consists of salient features of the study such as purpose, methodology, results and conclusion.

**(vii) Preparation of draft text**

This stage constitutes the preparation of the draft text by using the extracted information into a content that can be used most effectively and efficiently by users. This involves the arrangement of ideas or information in a helpful sequence and integrating the information collected into an organised text. For this purpose, it is necessary to prepare a document plan before attempting to write the draft.

The document plan should consist of :

(i) defining requirements which comprises subject overview, scope and purpose of the document, how it will be used, how the document relate to other documents, audience definition etc;

(ii) Outline preparation – consists of detailed listing of the major sections and subsections. In the development of a topical outline, the principle to be adopted must be compatible with the document objectives. Generally four main types of organising principles can be used for organising ideas in the content. They are Logical, chronological, psychological and topical organisation.

The extracts collected from various selected sources after analysis and arrangement of ideas in a sequence helpful to the users and with the appropriate orientation, are to be integrated into an organised text. For this purpose, the target audience and their intellectual level or standard, the intended use of information product, the impact one desires of the product on the audience, the peculiarities of the subject, users' preferences to a particular kind of presentation of information are some of the factors to be considered. The result of integration should conform to the principle of unity of ideas. In this process of integration, the objective of the information product should be kept in mind. The flow of ideas should be logical, step by step through the structural elements of the text. Also the presentation of information should be based on an optimal synchronising of textual and visual presentations.

Saracevic and Wood (1981) opine that restructuring and repackaging of information in the technical communications should be in consonance with communication practices of users on the one hand, and on the other should reliably reflect the state of knowledge or data on the given subject. They observe that more specifically, restructuring requires determination of :

- Extent to which available content is to be incorporated
- Degree of invariability of information as found in the original( i.e which new information value is to be added)
- Degree of detail in information
- Degree of changes in sequence of presentation relative to the original
- Technical sophistication
- Temporal presentation
- Editorial qualities.

The integration of information can be achieved by:

- Application of classificatory principles
- Adopting methods of presentation of information
- Following general rules of grammar, style etc involved in technical writing

- Orientation, if any, to the needs and levels of users
- Application of visual presentation technique.

There are two types of presentation of information in technical document : textual and non-textual or visual presentation. In the case of textual presentation, the text may differ according to the target audience to whom it is meant. Thus, the presentation of information and layout of the text may have to be altered depending upon the destination. In the textual presentation the tips of language are also to be followed in technical communication. Use of simple language, short sentences, use of less difficult words, use of jargon with discretion, use of active voice rather than passive voice, use of positive phrasing rather than negative phrasing, diction, grammar, spelling, punctuations etc should be followed for the effective communication of the information consolidated product. Whether non-textual presentations in the form of tables, diagrams, charts, graphs, etc are logically appropriately presented in the textual matter?

### (viii) Testing of draft

Evaluating the quality and effectiveness of the draft information consolidated product is the main activity of this stage. For this purpose the draft text is reviewed and assessed by subject experts and field tested by using it with end users. In the assessment of the draft by the subject experts the factors such as technical accuracy, completeness, perspective, analysis, synthesis organisation, appropriateness, value –added, utility etc are considered. While in the field testing the draft text facilitates improvement in the orientation of the text as well as ensures user acceptance and effectiveness of the document in the operating environment.

### (ix) Finalisation of the draft

The author finalises the text on the basis of the suggestions, proposed in the above stage. The suggestions or changes proposed may be in the form of addition or omission of information, sequence of ideas presented or changes in the visual presentation etc.

The format of the final information consolidated product comprises of three parts: Preliminaries, the body and auxiliaries.

The preliminary part consists of title page, summary or synopsis, contents page, list of table, list of figures, list of abbreviation, acknowledgement or introduction etc. The main body is organised under various sections. The auxiliaries comprise references, appendices, glossary etc

After the editorial work is completed, the manuscript should be handed over to the printing section/ reprographic section for the preparation of multiple copies. Here the technical writer should go through various stages of printing and publishing of the technical document in the final form.

### (x) Dissemination of information

Now the information consolidated document is ready for distribution. The diffusion or dissemination of information consolidated product will encourage and promote its use. This may also involve user education in the use of information and marketing of information.

### (xi) Feed back from users

The feedback from the users will provide necessary indices for ascertaining the validity of the information consolidated product.

## 7.6. EVALUATION OF INFORMATION PRODUCTS

The technical document may be sent to subject experts or specialists in the respective areas. The criteria or checklist suggested by Saracevic may be considered for evaluation.

- **Completeness** : the degree to which both the subject and the literature on the subject was covered.
- **Perspective:** Purpose, direction, orientation, the degree of appropriateness in relation to both a given subject and for

a given audience.

- **Analysis:** the thoroughness, depth and breadth of analysis, degree of collation from different sources, degree of evaluation applied in analysis.
- **Synthesis:** degree of compaction and relation drawn, extent of superseding of previous information and literature, power of inferences, degree of drawing from related subjects, degree of evaluation applied in synthesis.
- **Value-added :** identification of emerging specialities, introduction of new hypotheses or theories, suggestions for future work, serving as an inspiration, stimulus.
- **Utility :** the degree to which a review can serve multiple functions and not only one or two functions.

## 7.7. INFORMATION CONSOLIDATED PRODUCTS

In a library or information centre quite a good number of information consolidated products can be generated on demand or in anticipation. These include review articles, state-of the-art reports, Trend reports, Information digest, handbook etc. The steps followed for the generation of these products are more or less the same as those of steps followed in information consolidation discussed above.

### 7.71. Review Article.

A review article is a comprehensive and authoritative written presentation published in a journal, a monograph, a treatise, a book, an encyclopaedia or in conference proceedings, giving an overview of the developments taken place in one subject area within a certain limited period, say the preceding year(s). Review is a critical synthesis of the state of knowledge in a given subject or topic. In fact it is a critical examination of information and literature on a subject accommodated in a broader format. In the spectrum of many possible information consolidation products, reviews take a special and most significant place.

It was prepared earlier only by subject specialists, now it is being prepared also by information managers who have been trained in the techniques of information analysis and consolidation. The review article may be merely a descriptive bibliography of all papers on a subject, speculative, very close to primary literature, a promoter of some particular theory, a careful compilation of experimental data, an account of mathematical technique, bringing together and expounding implicit axioms, theorems, didactic meant for the beginners in the subject and a clear disposition of what is well known in a language intelligible to outsiders.

## TYPES

Review article can be categorised into i) Historical; ii) Descriptive; iii) Critical or evaluative; iv) popular ;v) Bibliographic; and vi) review alerts.

## Characteristics of Review article

A review article has the attributes such as the title or abstract which must contain any of the terms viz review, progress, survey, overview, advances, trends, state-of –the –report, status report etc. It contains several references. It generally appears in serials devoted entirely to reviews and is indexed in indexing and abstracting periodicals.

## Functions

There are two types of functions of reviews: historical and contemporary. Historical function is those which are fundamental to development of a subject or a topic. While contemporary function is those which are beneficial to individual users. Reviews can be deliberately structured to emphasise some of the functions and encourage some of the uses.

## Uses

As an information consolidated product, a review article has a number of uses. They are:

- It provides an insight into scientific progress made on a specific area.
- It caters scientist-to-scientists communication within a subject area.
- It serves as a current awareness tool.
- It aids planners and policy makers to fix national priorities.
- It alerts advance centres to introduce study programmes in new and upcoming areas of research.
- It helps R & D institutions to formulate policies and programmes of research.

Preparation of Review article

The methodology in the preparation of review article encompasses the following steps.

**(i) Ascertain the users' requirement** : Here the technical writer should enunciate the potential user /s in order to ascertain the pertinent requirements such as area or subject, scope, type of reviews etc.

**(ii) Selection of the specific topic** : In the selection of the topic, the writer should examine whether the topic is too broad or too narrow. Recency and significance of the topic are other aspects for consideration. For example ' Cloud computing: a review', User research: a status report', 'Progress of nanotechnology in India' 'Trends in webometric studies 'etc are some of the topics.

**(iii) Selection of type of review article** : On the basis of the information requirement of the user or user group the writer chooses the type of review article such as historical, critical, descriptive or bibliographical.

**(iv) Literature survey** : A comprehensive survey of the literature on the topic selected for preparation of the review article should be conducted in this stage. Documentary and non-documentary sources have to be consulted for this purpose. In the case of documentary sources an effective information search can be conducted from tertiary to secondary and secondary to primary sources. Non documentary sources like formal and human sources can also be consulted.

**(v) Selection of information sources :** An objective and judicious selection of information sources are used for the selection of the information sources collected in the above stage. In the selection of the information sources criteria such as authenticity, correctness and recency etc can be adopted.

**(vi) Analysis and Extraction :** Content analysis of the selected information sources are carried out here. Extract of each analysed source is prepared. Here the restructuring of the original document is carried out. The restructured information consists of citation of the source with extracted or abstract of the original source. The abstract contains elements like purpose, methods, results and conclusion in the case of a scientific article.

**(vii) Classification of the packaged items of information :** Here the packaged items can be organised or classified. For this purpose classification such as chronological, logical, psychological, topical etc can be selected on the basis of suitability of the topic and type of review. For organisation of information the writer should decide the main and sub-divisions of the review.

**(viii) Preparation of the preliminary draft :** Preliminary draft is prepared giving a broad framework containing information according to the pattern set by the writer and references at specific points to which reference applies.

**(ix) Re-assessment of the preliminary draft :** In the re-assessment stage the writer should examine, does it include a description presenting a statement or subject?; are all facts presented impartially?; is the organisation of ideas or information clear, logical and coherent? ; are all important points covered and emphasised? ; are there any gaps in the presentation?; will it be credible to the user? etc

**(x) Re-writing of the article :** The article is re-written after the reassessment of preliminary draft by the writer. The article is re-written paying attention to style of presentation, grammar and syntax. Appropriate tables and illustrations are prepared.

**(xi) Preparation of the second draft :** This draft is prepared in the standard format, incorporating references to tables, figures and citation at the appropriate places in the text. This draft also can be critically examined and modifications can be made.

**(xii) Finalisation of the draft :** The finalised draft comprises of three distinct areas viz preliminaries, the main body and auxiliaries in order. In the preliminaries area, information is organised as – title, abstract and key words, author statement ; in the main body the study is organised in sections; the auxiliaries consist of appendix and references. Finalised draft is printed

### 7.72. State- of- the- Art- Report/ Status Report/Trend Report

These are types of reviews which do not have an all-encompassing scope and historical orientation. This report is an exposition of a subject, giving an account of the general direction of research in the subject, based on a review of the documents on current developments. They emphasise recency and up-to-datedness. Their aim is to describe a very recent situation when they reach their audience. Thus they are more timely than the traditional review, so that they are mostly current awareness tools. In order to achieve this currency, these reports are often published as informal reports prepared on demand, oriented to a restricted audience. These reports are descriptive type of reviews usually prepared in the area of science and technology, commerce etc. Topics like 'Research on nanotechnology: A state of the Art Report', 'Library computerisation in India: A status report', ' Research on Space launch vehicles: A trend report' etc can be considered as some of the examples.

The methodology for the preparation of these information consolidated products is more or less the same as that of the steps discussed in the review article above. The format of the state-of the -art report or trend report is as follows:

Title page – consists of title of the report, name of the writer, Name and place of affiliating institution and year.

Executive summary – an informative abstract of the report is provided

Contents page

List of tables

List of Figures

List of abbreviations

The main Body -The Report

Appendix/es

References

Glossary

Index.

## REFERENCES

Bestide, F, et al (1989) The use of review articles in the analysis of research area. Scientometrics. 15 (5-6) PP.535-62

Herring, C(1968) Critical reviews: The users' point of view. J.Chem.Documenttion.8(4) pp.232-36.

Kumar, PSG(2004). Information analysis, repackaging, consolidation of information retrieval. New Delhi, B.R.Publications.

Rastogi, T( 1982). Consolidation of information : Wind pump: Handbook. Paris, UNESCO.

Saraceevic,Tefko(1986). A course in information consolidation: A handbook for education and training in analysis, synthesis and repackaging of information. Paris, UNESCO

Saracevic, T and Wood, J(1981) Consolidation of information : A handbook on evaluation, restructuring and repackaging of scientific and technical information. Paris, UNESCO.

Seetharama,S(1997) Information consolidation and repackaging. New Delhi, ESS ESS Publications.

UNESCO.(1984) Final report of the UNISIST working Group on information analysis and consolidation. Paris, UNESCO.

Virgo, JA (1971). The review article, its characteristics and problems.Lib.Qtly.41(4).pp275-91.

Woodward, AM (1977) The role of reviews in information transfer. J.Am.Soc.Inform.Sci.28(3).pp175-80.

# 8

# Editor, Editing, Editorial Tools and Proof Reading

## 8.1. INTRODUCTION

Any professional, whether technical writer, librarian, research scholar who, as part of his job, writes, evaluates or monitors informative text to make it readable, requires editing skills and can identify himself with the role of an editor. Though the task of the writer and editor seem distinct and separate, there is actually much overlap, as the writer does a lot of editing while revising his manuscript. Unless a writer is aware of and appreciates the role of the editor in the preparation of the manuscripts, his knowledge of his task as writer would remain incomplete.

Writers and editors produce a wide variety of written materials delivered to an audience in an increasing number of ways. They develop content using any number of multimedia formats for readers, listeners or viewers. Although many people write as part of their primary job, only writers and editors who are paid for their work are included in this occupation. Major news papers, news magazines, scholarly journals usually employ several types of editors such as executive editor, Managing editor, Chief editor, editor, assistant editor etc. Editor is one who edits manuscripts, especially as an occupation. The editor is the 'quality-control man' who gives the manuscripts the final shape and style in its printed form and acts as a buffer between the author and his reading public. He represents the 'invisible imprint' in all quality books which the reader rarely notices.

Written communication should be intelligible, clear and concise so that the reader gets the message intended by the writer without too many hurdles to comprehension. A manuscript has to go through various stages of processing for comprehension before being sent to the printer. This process is known as editing and one who executes the activities is known as editor. Once the manuscript is with the publisher, the editor becomes responsible for shaping the text for publication. Sometimes all that an editor is required to do is mark the manuscripts for concreteness of grammar, punctuation, headings, paragraphing and layout. Most often the editor does advise the author on style and content.

The role of editors are very significant in the present printed world. They act as moulders of a nation's literary tastes and setters of academic standards. They select manuscripts for publication, sign authors to produce texts for universities and schools, promote writers with unexplored talents, scour academic disciplines in which there is not enough published materials and search for and invite manuscripts for publication.

As a significant person in the publishing industry, editor should have the following qualities.

- a subject expert
- skilled in copy editing
- skilled in proof reading
- skilled in type setting and printing
- able to advise a writer on how to reorganise and rewrite weak portions of the text
- a manager of men and resources
- knowledgeable in the legal aspects of publishing
- responsible for public morals

- responsible for the quality of the book that is published
- a good sales person
- a very well read person
- able to manage the company's accounts
- a good administrator
- a marketing expert
- an intellectual and well informed.

As an editor he is expected to carry out a number of functions in the context of editorial policy, marketing, publicity, choice of manuscripts etc. Based on these, the functions of an editor can be summed up as given below.

- acquisition of manuscripts from authors
- assessment of manuscripts for scope, content and marketability
- seeking expert's opinions on the manuscripts
- processing the manuscripts for substantive editing, style editing and copy editing
- seeing the manuscripts through various stages of production and printing.

The above listing shows only some of the more important functions exemplifying the role of an editor. Unlike the editor of a magazine, journal or the general editor of a series, the editor in a book publishing house has to be critic, a cost accountant, a business executive, a visualiser and a public relation man, all rolled into one. Unless he enjoys doing such a variety of jobs, his usefulness to the publisher will be limited. In India such multi-purpose editors may be found with certain publishers but they end up by doing all the miscellaneous work of the organisation without any supporting staff. This again adversely affects their technical work as editors.

## 8.2. The Editor's skills

The skills required for an editor can be identified by the functions and responsibilities allotted to him. By considering the professional tasks of editor from acquisition of manuscript to the final production warrants certain essential skills. They are:

- The editor must be a well informed person generally, but particularly in the areas in which his publishing firm specialises
- The editor should be aware of book reviews and news/reports on the subject of his specialisation
- The editor should be acquainted with the legal aspects of book publishing
- He must have working knowledge of printing technology, typographic design, types and sizes of paper and categories of publication
- He must utilise the services of agencies such as national centre for ISBN and ISSN
- He must have essential knowledge of legal deposit requirements of the country
- The editor should be one trained in the knowledge and skills of editing

## 8.3. What is editing?

Editing is the process of selecting and preparing written, visual, audible and film media used to convey information through the process of correction, condensation, organisation, and other modifications performed with an intention of producing a correct, consistent, accurate and complete work. The editing process often begins after the author's work is created. As such, editing is a practice that includes creative skills, human relations, and a precise set of methods.

Evans has pointed out the following checklists or criteria for editing

(i) Conformity to specification headings
(ii) Page numbering
(iii) Paragraph numbering
(iv) Conformity of contents list to text
(v) Layout of illustrations as per specification
(vi) Unusual words of phrases
(vii) Unexplained abbreviations
(viii) Long words that may not be understood
(ix) Unnecessary words –adjectives, adverbs etc
(x) Undefined technical terms
(xi) Balance of text –length of paragraph etc
(xii) Ambiguities in flow of text
(xiii) Punctuation
(xiv) Grammatical construction
(xv) Spelling
(xvi) Conformity of meaning of text to what was intended

## Levels of Editing

According to Madhushree the technical editing constitutes three levels : They are:

- Editing the text for grammatical, spelling and style errors
- Editing the organisation of content, emphasis, appropriateness of content and adherence to standards and guidelines.
- Editing for the accuracy of content, visual presentation, formatting issues, errors in the table of contents and indexes that have not been updated.

## Types of Editing

The editing can be categorised into the following types

**(i) Developmental Editing** : Similar to ghost writing in collaboration with the author, a developmental editor assists the author as a writing coach by taking a rough draft of a manuscript from initial concept and make suggestions about content, organisation, and presentation. The developmental editor always has the target audience in mind and may make an analysis of competing works and suggest additional research to fish out certain parts and give the book credibility and factual content. Plot and characterisation will be analysed and reworked if needed. Suggestions will be given for rewriting confusing and awkward areas to create better flow. Sentence structure, punctuation, grammar and spelling may also be considered. In brief the following activities are involved in the developmental editing.

- Working with the client and, usually the author of a book or other document to develop a manuscript from initial concept, outline, or draft through any number of subsequent drafts
- Making suggestions about content, organisation, and presentation, based on analysis of competing works, comments of expert reviewers, the client's market analysis, and other appropriate references
- Rewriting, writing, and researching, as needed, and sometimes suggesting topics or providing information about topics for consideration of authors and client.

(ii) **Substantive Editing** : Substantive editing or Heavy editing improves a manuscript by identifying and solving problems with order and flow of information. It may require reorganising paragraphs, sections, or chapters for overall clarity and readability. Sentence structure, transitions, punctuations, grammar and spellings will also be considered. To sum up, the substantive editing constitutes the following activities

- Identifying and solving problems of overall clarity or accuracy
- Reorganising paragraphs, sections, or chapters to improve the order in which the text is presented

- Writing or rewriting segments of text to improve readability and flow of information
- Revising any or all aspects of the text to improve its presentation
- Consulting with others about issues of concern
- Incorporating responses to queries and suggestions creating a new draft of the document.

**(iii) Copy editing or line editing :** Clear presentation of the material for the typesetter involves making sure that it is complete and that all the parts are clearly identified: for example the grade of each subheading, which pieces of text should be distinguished typographically from the main text, and where tables and illustrations should be placed. The copy editor may also size the illustrations, mark type sizes, and so on.

The same person may do all four of these things, or they may be split in various ways. The main aims of copy-editing are to remove any obstacles between the reader and what the author wants to convey, and also to save time and money by finding and solving any problems before the book is typeset, so that production can go ahead without interruption. In fact the copy editing constitutes the following activities:

- Correcting spelling, grammar, punctuation, syntax, and word usage while preserving the meaning and voice of the original text
- Checking for or imposing a consistent style and format
- Preparing style sheet that documents style or format
- Reading for overall clarity and sense on behalf of the prospective audience
- Querying the appropriate party about apparent errors or inconsistencies
- Noting permissions needed to publish copyrighted material
- Preparing a manuscript for the next stage of the publication process

- Cross-checking references, art, figures, tables, equations, and other features for consistency with their mentions in the text.
- It has been said that the 'Five C's' constitute copy editor's job in order to make the copy
- Clear
- Correct
- Concise
- Comprehensible and
- Consistent.

The skills for copy editors include: an excellent command of language, general knowledge for spotting factual errors, good critical thinking skills in order to recognise inconsistencies, interpersonal skills for interaction with writers and other copy editors, and a sense of style.

## Editorial process

Let us consider what happens when a text is being processed for publication and the role of the editor in this undertaking. The editorial processes of a manuscript would follow the following stages.

**(i) Author's draft given to editor** : The editorial process commences only after the author gives his manuscript to the editor. The editor should exercise his skills in the selection of the manuscript for the publication. After reading a few pages or so of a manuscript the editor can decide whether to accept or reject it at the outset. Once he accepts it he goes through the manuscript in detail keeping the criteria for selection in mind. In the case of scientific and technical publications it is the responsibility of the editor to maintain the quality and standard of the publication.

**(ii) Evaluation by peer groups** : Once the manuscript is provisionally selected by the editor it should undergo review by experts in the field. For this the manuscript should be sent to two to three peer reviewers as per the editorial policy of the publishing firm for their opinion relating to the authenticity, quality and standard of the article /book for the publication. The reviewers use structured procedures for commenting and evaluating a manuscript. A copy of the manuscript is sent to the reviewer with a rating form which states the criteria and scale on which the reviewer has to base his judgement. The reviewer communicates with the editor within the time period assigned for the evaluation. The editor gets the reviews from all the experts or peers. If these are fairly similar he combines them into a single report and sends it to author as his own decision. The final decision of the editor depends on the majority opinion of the peers..

**(iii) Content editor's and Language editors' comments** : After the acceptance of the manuscript by the peers the manuscript t should be sent for the content editor's and language editor's comments. The content editor will go through the manuscript with an objective of the content organisation of the manuscript while the language editor will consider the language aspect such as grammar, spelling, diction etc in the manuscript and record their remarks relating to the manuscript.

**(iv) Author-Editor Interaction** : In the light of the remarks of the peer groups, content editor's and language editor's comments, author- editor interaction is carried out through correspondence.

**(v) Revision of the Text** : Revision of the manuscript is carried out based on the remarks of the peer reviewers, content editors, language editors and based on author –editor interaction.

**(vi) Stylistic and Format changes by Editor** : After the revision of the manuscript stylistic and format changes are made by the editor as per stipulation of the publishing firm

**(vii) Final product reviewed by Author** : The final corrected or modified manuscript will again sent to the author for perusal

**(viii) Press ready Manuscript** : The approved manuscript by the author is the press ready copy for printing

## 8.4. EDITORIAL TOOLS

In the process of editing, the editor uses a number of tools. These are :

- Dictionaries
- Thesaurus
- Style manuals
- Standards etc

### Dictionaries

Dictionaries are reference tools containing an alphabetical list of words with information given for each word, usually including, meaning, pronunciation, etymology, spelling, capitalisation, different uses of words, abbreviations, synonyms and antonyms, translations into another language etc. There are various types of dictionaries used in editorial section. They include: General language dictionaries, Subject Dictionaries and special Dictionaries.

*Examples*

The Oxford English Dictionary by J.A Simpson and ESC Weiner. Oxford Clarendon Press

Webster's Third New International Dictionary of the English Language. Springfield, Mass, Merriam Webster.

Merriam- Webster on-line Dictionary

Longman English Dictionary

Chamber's Dictionary

Russian English Dictionary

Russian English Malayalam Dictionary

McGraw-Hill Dictionary of Science and Technology

Medical Dictionary

Dictionary of abbreviations

The Oxford Dictionary of quotations

Familiar quotations by John Bartlet

The Australian Slang Dictionary

Dictionary of Proverbs

## Thesaurus

Thesaurus literally means a treasure. In a thesaurus words carrying the same meaning and other related terms are listed and the nuances in meaning and usage are described.. Roget's thesaurus of English words and phrases composed by B. Kirkpatrick and Webster's Collegiate Thesaurus by Merriam Webster are two well known English language thesauri.

## Standards

In the context of technical editing, standards play an important role in relation to presentation of information in an appropriate manner. In India Bureau of Indian Standards and at the international level, International Standards Organisation(ISO) have brought out quite a good number of standards relevant to editing.. Bureau of Indian standards have published a number of standards for documentation pertaining to bibliographical reference, books and periodicals, proof corrections, typography etc Some of the examples are given below :

| Title | IS.No |
|---|---|
| Bibliographical Reference: Recommendations for bibliographic reference | 2381-1963 |
| General structure of preliminary pages of a book | 790-1956 |
| Guide for abbreviation of words in title of periodicals using Roman alphabet | 18-1970 |
| Guide for layout of Learned periodicals | 4-1963 |
| Guide for preparation of manuscript of an article in a learned periodical | 4731-1968 |
| Half title leaf of a book | 791-1956 |
| Practice for table of Contents | 794-1956 |
| Title page and back of title page | 792-1964 |

| | |
|---|---|
| Practice for Alphabetical arrangement | 382-1952 |
| Rules for making alphabetical indexes | 1275-1958 |
| Specification for Library Catalogue & Abstract card | 7150-1974 |
| Proof Corrections for Printers and Authors | 1250-1958 |
| Guide for selection of type and page lay out in text books | 6298-1971 |

## Style Manuals

A style manual is a set of standards for design and writing of documents, either for general use or for a specific publication or organisation. The implementation of a style manual provides uniformity in style and formatting of a document. Website style guides focus on a publication's visual and technical aspects, prose style, best usage, grammar, punctuation, spelling and fairness.. For the purpose of style editing the following style manuals would be useful.

### APA Style Manual

American Psychological Association(APA) style is a set of rules that authors use when submitting papers for publications in APA journal. The APA states that they were developed to assist reading comprehension in the social and behavioural sciences, for clarity of communication and to move the ideas forward with a minimum of distraction and a maximum of precision. The APA style manual contains guidelines for every aspect of writing, especially in the social sciences, from determining authorship to constructing a table to avoiding plagiarism and constructing accurate reference citations.

### The Chicago Manual of Style on line

The Chicago style manual is available in hard copy form and on on-line. The 16$^{th}$ edition of The Manual of Style is now available in on line. With state of the art recommendations on editorial style and publishing practices in the digital age, the Chicago manual of style is the must have reference tool for every one who works with words.

**Wikipedia: Manual of Style**

The manual of style (MOS) is a style for all Wikipedia articles. The MOS also comprises many sub pages which provide detailed guidance of on particular topic or subject areas. The MOS presents Wikipedia's house style, to help editors produce articles with consistent, clear, and precise language, lay out, and formatting. The major goal is to make the encyclopedia easier and more intuitive to use. Consistency in language, style, and formatting promote clarity and cohesion which is especially important within an article.

**MLA Handbook for Writers of Research papers**

The Modern Language Association (MLA) style manual is a handbook for writers of research papers.

**AAA (American Anthropological Association) Style**

The American Anthropological Association(AAA) Style format uses the Chicago Manual of Style and Webster's Tenth New Collegiate Dictionary.

**ASA(American Sociological Association) Style**

The American Sociological Association (ASA) Style is meant for the format preparation in sociology subject.

**CSE(Council of Science Editors) Style**

Council of Science Editors (CSE) Style was formerly known as Council of Biology Editors(CBE) meant for scientific format and style.

**Style Guides of ISO**

The International Standard Organisation (ISO) has brought out the following style guides in the areas of publication and documentation

**ISO 214** : Abstracts for publication and Documentation

**ISO :215** : Presentation of contributions to periodicals and other serials

**ISO 690** : Bibliographical references, content, forum and structure

**ISO 7144**: Presentation of the theses and similar documents

## 8.5. PROOF READING

Proof reading traditionally means reading a proof copy of a text in order to detect and correct errors. It is comparing the latest stage of text, marking discrepancies in text, and, when appropriate, checking for problems in page makeup, layout, colour separation, or type. Proof reading may also include one or more of the following activities:

- Checking proof against typesetting specifications
- Querying or correcting errors or inconsistencies that may have escaped an editor or writer
- Reading for typographical errors or for sense without reading against copy.

The following is a list of popularly used proof reading marks or symbols.

## Proof Readers' Symbols

| Symbol | Meaning | Example |
|---|---|---|
| ℊ or γ or ♂ | Delete | take it out |
| ⁀‿ | close up | print as o ne word |
| ℊ with ⁀‿ | delete and close up | cloose up |
| ∧ or > or ⅄ | Caret | insert here (something |
| # | insert a space | put onehere |
| eq# | space evenly | space evenly where indicated |
| stet | let stand | let marked text stand as set |
| tr | Transpose | change order the |
| / | used to separate two or more marks and often as a concluding stroke at the end of an insertion | |
| [ | set farther to the left | [ too far to the right |
| ] | set farther to the right | too] far to the left |
| ⌒ | set as ligature (such as æ) | encyclopaedia |
| = | align horizontally | alignment |
| ‖ | align vertically | ‖ align with surrounding text |
| x | broken character | imperfect |
| □ | indent or insert em quad space | |
| ¶ | begin a new paragraph | |
| (SP) | spell out | set (5 lbs.) as five pounds |
| cap | set in CAPITALS | set nato as NATO |
| sm cap or s.c. | set in SMALL CAPITALS | set signal as SIGNAL |

| | | |
|---|---|---|
| lc | set in lowercase | set South as south |
| ital | set in *italic* | set oeuvre as *oeuvre* |
| rom | set in roman | set *mensch* as mensch |
| bf | set in **boldface** | set important as **important** |
| = or -/ or ⌃ or /H/ | Hyphen | multi-colored |
| 1/N or en or /N/ | en dash | 1965–72 |
| 1/M or em or /M/ | em (or long) dash | Now—at last!—we know. |
| ∨ | superscript or superior | 2 as in $\pi r^2$ |
| ∧ | subscript or inferior | 2 as in $H_20$ |
| ⌃⌄ or ⌄⌃ | Centered | for a centered dot in $p \cdot q$ |
| ⌃,⌃ | Comma | |
| ⌄'⌄ | apostrophe | |
| ⊙ | Period | |
| ; or ;/ | Semicolon | |
| : or (:) | Colon | |
| “ ” or ' ' | quotation marks | |
| (/) | parentheses | |
| [/] | Brackets | |
| OK/? | query to author: has this been set as intended? | |
| ⊥ or ⊥[1] | push down a work-up | an unintended mark |
| 9[1] | turn over an inverted letter | inverted |
| wf[1] | wrong font | wrong size or style |

## REFERENCES


Butcher, Judith(2006). Copy-editing . The Cambridge handbook for editors, authors and publishers. London, Cambridge University Press.

EvansJ(1983) . Beginner's Guide to Technical writing. Butterworth &CO.

# Bibliography


Adelstein, Michael. *Contemporary Business Writing.* New York: Random House, 1971.

Alexander, Heather, and Ben Potter. "Case Study: The Use of Formal Specification and Rapid Prototyping to Establish Product Feasibility." *Information and Software Technology* 29.7 (1987): 388-394.

Alice Walker, "Everyday Use (for your grandmamma)." In Love & Trouble: Stories of Black Women by Alice Walker, reprinted by permission of Harcourt Brace & Company.

Allison, B. *The Student's Guide to Preparing Dissertations and Theses.* London: Kogan Page. 1997.

American Chemical Society. *Handbook for Authors.* Washington, D.C.: American Chemical Society, 1967.

American Institute of Physics. *Style Manual,* rev.ed. New York: American Institute of Physics. 1973.

American Medical Association. *Stylebook/Editorial Manual,* 5th ed. Chicago: American Medical Association, 1971.

American National Standards Institute (ANSI). *American National Standard for Writing Abstracts* (Z39. 14-1979). New York: ANSI, 1979.

American National Standards Institute. *Guidelines for Format and Production of Scientific and Technical Reports.* [ANSI 239. 18-1974]. New York: Author, 1974.

Anderson, G. and Arsenault, N. *Fundamentals of Educational Research,* 2nd edn. London: Falmer. 1998

Andrea Lunsford and Lisa Ed, *Singular Texts/Plural Authors: Perspective on Collaborative Writing.* Carbondale and Edwardsville, IL: Southern Illinois University Press, 1992, pp. 45-48.

Angelo, Rocco M. *Understanding Feasibility Studies.* East Lansing, MI: Educational Institute of the American Hotel and Motel Association, 1985.

Annie Dillard, "Living Like Weasels," in *Teaching a Stone to Talk:* Expeditions and Encounters. by Annie Dillard. Reprinted with the permission of Harper Collins Publishers, Inc. 1982

Arksey, H. and Knight, P. (1999) *Interviewing for Social Scientists: An Introductory Resource with Examples.* London: Sage.

Article abstract of "Midlife Myths" by Winfred Gallagher, May 1993. Abstract reprinted with the permission of *The Atlantic Monthly.*

Bacon, Terry. "Selling the Sizzle, Not the Steak: Writing Customer-Oriented Proposals." *Proceedings of the First National Conference on Effective Communication Skills for Technical Professionals.* Greenville, SC: Continuing Engineering Education, Clemson University, November 15-16, 1988.

Bailey, C.A.. *A Guide to Field Research.* Thousand Oaks, CA: Pine Forge Press.1996

Barnes, R. *Successful Study for Degrees.* London: Routledge.1995

Barzun, Jacques. *Simple and Direct: A Rhetoric for Writers.* New York: Harper & Row, 1975.

Beardsley, Monroe C. *Thinking Straight:* Principles of Reasoning for Readers and Writers, 4th ed. Englewood Cliffs, N.J.: Prentice-Hall, 1975.

Beck, Charles E., and John A. Stribravy. "Word Processing as an Investment in Quality." *Word Processing for Technical Writers.* Ed. Robert Krull. Amityville, NY: Baywood, 1988. 20-30.

Bell Telephone Laboratories. *Editorial Style Guide.* Whippany, N.J.: Bell Telephone Laboratories, 1961.

Berger, A.A. *Improving Writing Skills: Memos, Letters, Reports and Proposals.* London: Sage. 1993

Beveridge, W.I.B. *The Art of Scientific Investigation,* rev.ed. New York: Norton, 1957.

Bill Russell. Excerpt from Second Wind: *The Memoirs of an Opinionated Man* by Bill Russell with Taylor Branch. New York: Random House, 1979. by William F. Russell. Reprinted with the permission of The Robbins Office.

Bradford, Annette. "Learning to Write with a Word Processor." *Word Processing for Technical Writers.* Ed. Robert Krull. Amityville, NY: Baywood, 1988. 160-169.

Bradford, Michael. "Four Types of Feasibility Studies Can Be Used." Business Insurance June 19, 1989: 16.

Brause, R.S. *Writing your Doctoral Dissertation: Invisible Rules for Success.* London: Falmer. 2000.

British Standards Institution (1990) *Recommendations for Citing and Referencing Published Material.* BS 5605. London: British Standards Institution.

Brown, A. *Gaining a Master's Degree.* Oxford: How to Books.1997

Brusaw, Charles T., et al. *Handbook of Technical Writing.* New York: St. Martin's, 1976.

Bryant Stamford, "Understand Calories, Fat Content in Food," *Seattle Times,* July 27, 1995..

Bryman, A. and Burgess, R.G. ed. *Analysing Qualitative Data.* London: Routledge.1994

Burnett, Rebecca E. "Substantive Conflict in a Cooperative Conflict: A Way to Improve the Collaborative Planning of a Workplace Document." *Technical Communication* 38.4 (Fourth Quarter 1991): 532-539.

Business Roundtable. "The Rationale for Ethical Corporate Behaviour." *Business Ethics 90/90.* Ed. John E. Richardson.

Guilford, CT: Dushkin, 1989. 204-207. Originally published in *Business and Society Review* XX (1988): 33-36.

Butcher, Judith. Copy editing: The Cambridge handbook for editors, authors and publishers.London, Cambridge University Press,1992

Carroll, John, et al. "Exploring a Wordprocessor." Effective Documentation: What We Have Learned From Research. Ed. Stephen Doheny-Farina. Cambridge, MA: MIT, 1988. 103-126.

Clough, P. and Nutbrown, C. *A Student's Guide to Methodology:* Justifying Enquiry. London: Sage.2002

Cohen, Gerald and Donald H. Cunningham. *Creating Technical Manuals: A Step-by-Step Approach to Writing User-Friendly Manuals.* New York: McGraw-Hill, 1984.

Collins, Belinda, et al. *A New Look at Windows.* NBSIR 77-1388. Washington, DC: National Bureau of Standards, 1978.

Cook, Marshall, and Blake R. Kellogg. *The Brochure: How to Write and Design it.* Madison, WI, 1980.

Corbett, Edward P.J. *Classical Rhetoric for the Modern Student.* New York: Oxford University Press, 1965.

Corby Kummer, "Is Coffee Harmful?" The Atlantic Monthly, July 1990..

Council of Biology Editors. *Style Manual,* 3rd ed. Washington, D.C.: American Institute of Biological Sciences, 1972.

Crème, P. and Lea, M.R. *Writing at University: A Guide for Students.* Buckingham: Open University Press.,1997

Creswell, J.W. *Qualitative Inquiry and Research Design: Choosing among Five Traditions.* Thousand Oaks, CA: Sage. 1998

Cryer, P. *The Research Student's Guide to Success.* Buckingham: Open University Press.1996

David S. Bennahum, "Getting Cyber Smart." *The New York Times,* May 22, 1995.

Debs, Mary Beth. "Recent Research on Collaborative Writing in Industry." *Technical Communication* 38.4 (Fourth Quarter 1991): 476-484.

Delamont, S., et al. *Supervising the PhD: A Guide to Success.* Buckingham: The Society for Research into Higher Education and Open University Press.1997

Denscombe, M.. *Ground Rules for Good Research: A 10 Point Guide for Social Researches.* Buckingham: Open University Press. 2002

Dey, I.. *Qualitative Data Analysis: A User-friendly Guide for Social Scientists.* London: Routledge. 1993

Dodd, Janet S., ed. *The ACS Style Guide: A Manual for Authors and Editors.* Washington, DC: American Chemical Society, 1986.

Dorff, Diane Lee, and Ann Hill Duin. "Applying a Cognitive Model to Document Cycling." *The Technical Writing Teacher* 16.3.1989: 234-249.

Drew, S. and Bingham, R.. *The Student Skills Guide,* 2nd edn. Sheffield: Sheffield Hallam University. 2001

Driskill, Linda. "Understanding the Writing Context in Organizations." *Writing in the Business Professions.* Ed. Myra Kogen. Urbana, IL: NCTE, 1989. 125-145.

Duin, Ann Hill. "How People Read: Implications for Writers. "*The Technical Writing Teacher* 15.3 1988: 185-193.

Edward Abbey, "The Damnation of a Canyon," in *Beyond the Wall: Essays from the Outside* by Edward Abbey, by Edward Abbey. Reprinted by permission of Henry Holt and Co., Inc. 1984

Eric Konigsberg, "Dad Always Liked You Best," GQ, June 1995, p. 48.

Erickson, B.H. and Nosanchuk, T.A.. *Understanding Data,* 2nd edn. Buckingham: Open University Press. 1992

Evans, J. Beginner's Guide to Technical Writing. Butterworths &

co, 1993

Fahnestock, Jeanne, and Marie Secor. *A Rhetoric of Argument.* New York: Random House, 1982.

Fairbairn, G.J. and Winch, C. Reading, Writing and Reasoning: *A Guide for Students.* Buckingham: The Society for Research into Higher Education, and Open University Press. 1991.

Fenno, Charles R. "Strategies for Word Processing in Technical Communication." *Word Processing for Technical Writers.* Ed. Robert Krull. Amityville, NY: Baywood, 1988. 47-60.

Fielden, John S. "What Do You Mean You Don't Like My Style?" *Harvard Business Review* 60 (1982): 128-138.

Finney, Paul R. "A Layman's Guide to Network Bafflegab (A Glossary)," *Management Technology* July 1983: 28.

Flick, U.. *An Introduction to Qualitative Research.* London: Sage.

Florence King. "I'd Rather Smoke Than Kiss," *National Review,* July 9, 1990, pp. 32-36..

Flower, Linda. "Rhetorical Problem Solving: Cognition and Professional Writing." *Writing in the Business Professions.* Ed. Myra Kogen. Urbana, IL: NCTE, 1989. 3-36.

Gash, S. (1989) *Effective Literature Searching for Students.* Aldershot: Gower.

General Electric Company. *Style Manual for Technical Writers.* N.p.: General Electric, 1964.

Gillian Dyer, "On Manner and Activity." In *Advertising as Communication.* by Gillian Dyer. Reprinted with the permission of Methuen & Co., International Thomson Publishing Services, Andover, UK. 1982

Glaser, B.G. and Strauss, A.L.. *The Discovery of Grounded Theory.* New York: Aldine de Gruyter. 1967

Goswami, Dixie, et al. *Writing in the Professions: A course Guide and Instructional Materials for an Advanced Composition Course.* Washington, DC: American Institute for Research, 1981.

Gravey, WD. Communication: The essence of science facilitating information exchange among libraries, scientists, engineers and students. Oxford, Pergamon press, 1979.

Green, Georgia M. "Linguistics and the Pragmatics of Language Use." *Poetics* 11 (1982):45-76.

Griffin, Jack. "When Do Rhetorical Choices Become Ethical Choices?" *Technical Communication and Ethics.* Ed. R. John Brockman and Fern Rook. Arlington, VA: Society for Technical Communication, 1989, 63-70. Originally published in *Proceedings of the 27th International Technical Communication Conference* (Washington: STC, 1980).

Hall, Dean G., and Bonnie A. Nelson. "Integrating Professional Ethics into the Technical Writing Course." *Journal of Technical Writing and Communication* 17.1 (1987): 45-61. Exercises 5-7 are based on material from this article.

Hannah, Arendt. *The Human Condition. Chicago:* University of Chicago Press, 1958.

Harcourt, Jules. "Developing Ethical Messages: A Unit of Instruction for the Basic Business Communication Course." *The Bulletin of the Association for Business Communication* 53 (1990): 17-20.

Hartley, Peter. "Writing for Industry: The Presentational Mode Versus the Reflective Mode." *The Technical Writing Teacher* 18.2 (1991): 162-169.

Hayakawa, S.I. *Language in Thought and Action,* 3rd ed. New York: Harcourt Brace Jovanovich, 1972.

Heid, Jim. "Getting Started with Choosing a Mac." *MacWorld January* 1992:

Holcombe, Marya W., and Judith K. Stein. *Writing for Decision Makers: Memos and Reports with a Competitive Edge.* Belmont, CA: Lifelong, 1981.

Holmes, Nigel. "Get Smart About Charts." *Publish!* 4.3 (1989): 42-45.

Honeywell. *Air Data/Inertial Reference System (ADIRS).* Minneapolis, MN: Honey-well, 1984.

Howard Gardner, *The Mind's New Science: A History of the Cognitive Revolution.* New York: Basic Books, 1985.

Huckin, Thomas. "A Cognitive Approach to Readability." *New Essays in Technical and Scientific Communication: Research, Theory, Practice.* Ed. Paul V. Anderson, R. John

Brockman, and Carolyn R. Miller. Farmingdale, NY: Baywood, 1983. 90-108.

Jaehn, Alfred H. "Al." "How to Effectively Communicate with Data Tables." *Tappi Journal 70* (November 1987): 183-184.

James Jones, quoted in Jon Winokur, Ed., *Writers on Writing.* Philadelphia: Running Press, 1986.

James Moffett, *Active Voice: A Writing Program Across the Curriculum.* Montclair, NJ: Boynton/Cook Publishers, 1981.

Jonathan Swift, "A Modest Proposal." in *The Prose Works of Jonathan Swift.* London: Bell, 1914.

Jonathan Swift,, quoted in Jon Winokur (Ed.)' *Writers on Writing.* Philadelphia: Running Press, 1986.

Jordan, Michael P. *Fundamentals of Technical Description.* Malabar, FL: Robert E. Krieger, 1984.

Kapp, Reginald O. *The Presentation of Technical Information.* New York: Macmillan, 1972.

Kenneth Burke, *The Grammar of Motives.* Berkeley: University of California Press, 1969.

Killingsworth, M. Jimmie and Michael Gilbertson. "How Can Text and Graphics Be Integrated Effectively?" *Solving Problems in Technical Writing.* Ed. Lynn Beene and Peter While. New York: Oxford, 1988. 130-149.

Kostelnick, Charles. "The Rhetoric of Text Design in Professional Communication." *The Technical Writing Teacher* 17.3 (1990): 189-203.

Krull, Robert. "Using Electronic Writing Aids." *Word Processing for Technical Writers.* Ed. Robert Krull. Amityville, NY: Baywood, 1988. 61-71.

Lay, Mary. "Nonrhetorical Elements of Layout and Design." *Technical Writing: Theory and Practice.* Ed. Bertie E. Fearing and W. Keats Sparrow. New York: MLA, 1989. 72-85.

Leonard, D. *A Woman's Guide to Doctoral Studies.* Buckingham: Open University Press. 2001

Levine, Linda, et al. "Implementing the Writing Plan: Heuristics from Software Development." *The Technical Writing Teacher,* 18.2 (1991): 116-125.

Lowell Ponte, "Earthquakes: Closer Than You Think," *Reader's Digest,* April 1994.

MacDonald-Ross, M. "Graphics in Texts." *Review of Research in Education.* Vol. 5. Ed. L.S. Shulman. Itasca, IL: F.E. Peacock, 1978.

Maizell, Robert E., et al. *Abstracting Scientific and Technical Literature.* New York: Wiley-Inter science, 1971.

Maker, J. and Lenier, M. *Academic Reading with Active Critical Thinking.* Belmont, CA: Wadsworth. 1996

Markel, Mike. "Criteria Development and the Myth of Objectivity." *The Technical Writing Teacher* 18.1 (Winter 1991): 37-47.

Martin, Harold C., and Richard M. Ohmann. *The Logic and Rhetoric of Exposition,* rev.ed. New York: Holt, 1965.

Mathes, J.C. "Assuming Responsibility: An Affective Objective in Teaching Technical Writing." *Technical Communication and Ethics.* Ed. R. John Brockman and Fern Rook. Arlington, VA: Society for Technical Communication, 1989. 89-90. Originally published in *Proceedings of the Technical Communication Sessions at the 32nd Annual Meeting of the Conference on College Composition and Communication.* (Dallas, TX: N.A.S.A Publication 2003, 1981).

Mathes, J.C., and Dwight W. Stevenson. *Designing Technical Reports*. Indianapolis: Bobbs-Merrill, 1976.

Mc Teague, Michael. "How to Write Effective Reports and Proposals." *Training and Development Journal* (Nov. 1988): 51-53.

Menzel, Donald H.,et al. *Writing a Technical Paper*. New York: McGraw-Hill, 1961.

Meenakshi Raman and Sangheeta Sharma. Technical communication: Principles and practice.New Delhi, Oxford Unversity Press, 2004.

Michel F. Graves and Wayne H. Slater, "Could Textbooks Be Better Written and Would It Make a Difference?" *American Educator*, Spring,1986, 36-42.

Miller, Tim. "Increasing Your Business I.Q. with On-line Data." Popular Computing Dec. 1985: 57+.

Mills, Gordon H., and John A. Walter. *Technical Writing*, 3rd ed. New York: Holt, 1970.

Mirel, Barbara, et al. "Designing Manuals for Active Learning Styles." *Technical Communication* 38.1 (1991): 75-87.

Mitchell, John H. *Writing for Professional and Technical Journals*. New York: Wiley, 1968.

Mulcahy, Patricia. "Writing Reader-Based Instructions: Strategies to Build Coherence." *The Technical Writing Teacher* 15.3 (1988). 234-243.

Neelameghan, A. *Presentation of Ideas in Technical Writing*. Delhi, Vikas Publishing House.1975

Odell, Lee, Dixie Goswami, Ann Herrington, and Doris Quick. "Studying Writing in Non-Academic Settings." *New Essays in Technical and Scientific Communication: Research, Theory and Practice*. Ed. Paul V. Anderson, R. John Brockman, Carolyn Miller, Farmingdale, NY: Baywood, 1983. 17-40.

Parker Palmer, *To Know as We Are Known: Education as a Spiritual Journey.* San Francisco: Harper and Row, 1983.

Pauley, Steven, E. and Riordan, Daniel, G.. *Technical Report Writing Today.* Delhi, A.I.T.B.S. Publishers & Distributors. 1996

Peter Elbow, *Writing Without Teachers.* New York: Oxford University Press, 1973,.

Phillips, E.M. and Pugh, D.S.. *How to Get a Ph.D Buckingham:* Open University Press. 2000.

Preece, R. *Starting Research: An Introduction to Academic Research and Dissertation Writing.* London: Continuum. 1994

*Publication Manual of the American Psychological Association.* 3rd ed. Washington, DC: APA, 1983.

Punch, K.F. *Introduction to Social Research.* London: Sage 1998.

Ramage, John D. and Bean, John C., *Guide to Writing Topic Edition.* America: Simon & Schuster Custom Publishing. 1997.

Redish,C. *Guidelines for Document Designers.* Washington, DC: American Institutes for Research, 1981.

Reddish, Janice. "Writing in Organizations." *Writing in the Business Professions.* Ed Myra Kogan. Urbana, IL: NCTE, 1989. 97-124.

Redish, Virginia. "Writing for People Who Are 'Reading to Learn to Do.'" *Creating Usable Manuals and Forms: A Document Design Symposium.* Technical Report 42. Pittsburgh, PA: Carnegie Mellon Communications Design Center, 1988.

Reimold, Cheryl. "The Trip Report Part 1: Preparation." *The Tappi Journal* 69.10 (1986): 168.

Riney, Larry A. *Technical Writing for Industry: An Operations Manual for the Technical Writer.* Englewood Cliffs, NJ: Prentice-Hall, 1989.

Rubens, Phillip M. "A Reader's View of Text and Graphics: Implications for Transactional Text." *Journal of Technical Writing and Communication* 16 (1986): 73-86.

Rubens, Phillip M. "A Reader's View of Text and Graphics: Implications for Transactional Text." *Journal of Technical Writing and Communication* 16.1/2 (1986): 73-86.

Rude, Carolyn D. "Format in Instruction Manuals: Applications of Existing Research." *Journal of Business and Technical Communication* 2 (1988): 63-77.

Rudestam, K.E. and Newton, R.R. *Surviving your Dissertation: A Comprehensive Guide to Content and Process.* Newbury Park, CA: Sage.1992

Sadowski, Mary A. "Elements of Composition." *Technical Communication* 34. (1987): 29-30.

Sapsford, R. and Jupp, V, ed *Data Collection and Analysis.* London: Sage. 1996

Saracevic, T and Wood,JS. Consolidation of information : A handbook of evaluation, restructuring and repackaging of scientific and technical information. Paris, UNESCO, 1981.

Schriver, Karen. *Teaching Writing to Anticipate the Reader's Needs:* A Classroom Evaluated Pedagogy. Technical Report Series, No. 46. Pittsburgh: Camegie-Mellon Communication Design Center, 1989.

Selzer, Jack. "Composing Process for Technical Discourse." *Technical Writing:* Theory and Practice. Ed. Bertie E. Fearing and W. Keats Sparrow. New York: MLA, 1989..

Selzer, Jack. "Composing Processes for Technical Discourse." *Technical Writing: Theory and Practice.* Ed. Bertie E. Fearing and W. Keats Sparrow. New York: MLA, 1989.

Seetharama,S. Information consolidation & repackaging. New Delhi, ESS ESS, 1997..

Sharp, J.A. and Howard, K., *The Management of a Student Research Project,* 2nd edn. Aldershot: Gower. 1996.

Shimberg, Lee H. "Ethics and Rhetoric in Technical Writing." *Technical Communication and Ethics.* Ed. R. John Brockman and Fern Rook. Arlington, VA: Society for Technical

Communication, 1989. 54-62. Originally published in Technical Communication 25 (Fourth Quarter 1978).

Silbergh, D.M.. Doing Dissertation in Politics: A Student Guide. London: Routledge. 2001

Slater, Wayne H. "Current Theory and Research on What Constitutes Readable Expository Text." *The Technical Writing Teacher* 15.3 (1988): 195-206.

Southard, Sherry. "Practical Considerations in Formatting Manuals." *Technical Communication* 35.3 (1988): 173-178.

Spinks, Nelda, and Barron Wells. "Employment Interviews: Trends in the Fortune 500 Companies – 1980-1988." *The Bulletin of the Association for Business Communications.* 51.4 (1988): 15-21.

Spivey, Nancy Nelson, and James R. King. "Readers as Writers Composing From Sources." *Reading Research Quarterly* Winter 1989: 7-26.

Stephen D. Brookfield, Developing Critical Thinkers: *Challenging Adults to Explore Alternative Ways of Thinking and Acting.* San Francisco: Jossey-Bass, 1987,.

Strunk, William, and White, E.B. *The Elements of Style,* 2nd ed. New York: Macmillan, 1972.

Sudol, Ronald A. "Applied Word Processing Notes on Authority, Responsibility, and

Revision in a Workshop Model." *College Composition and Communication* 36.3 (Oct. 1985): 331-335.

Tichy, H.J. *Effective Writing for Engineers, Managers, Scientists.* New York: Wiley, 1966.

Tom Wolfe, "New Journalism," introduction to *New Journalism,* Tome Wolfe and E.W. Johnson, Eds. New York: Harper & Row, 1973,.

Trelease, Sam F. *How to Write Scientific and Technical Papers.* Cambridge, Mass.: M.I.T. Press, 1969.

Treweek, David John, "Designing the Technical Communication Resume." *Technical Communications.* 38.2 (1991): 257-260.

Tufte, Edward R. *The Visual Display of Quantitative Information.* Cheshire, CT: Graphics Press, 1983.

Turabian, K.L.,. *A Manual for Writers of Term Papers, Theses and Dissertations,* 6th edn. Chicago, IL: University of Chicago Press.1996

Turner, BT. Effective technical writing and speaking.London, Business Books Ltd, 1974.

U.S. Government Printing Office. *Style Manual,* rev, ed. Washington, E.C.: U.S. Government Printing Office, 1973.

U.S. Treasury Department. *Effective Revenue Writing 2,* rev. ed. Washington, E.C.: U.S. Government Printing Office, 1962.

Ulman, Joseph N., Jr., and Jay R. Gould. *Technical Reporting,* 3rd ed. New York: Holt, 1972.

Vaughan, David K. "Abstracts and Summaries: Some Clarifying Distinctions." *The Technical Writing Teacher* 18.2 (1991): 132-141.

Wallace, John D., and J. Brewster Holding. *Guide to Writing and Style.* Columbus, Ohio: Battelle Memorial Institute, 1966.

Waller, Gary, et al. *The Lexington Introduction to Literature: Reading and Responding to Texts.* Lexington, MA:D.C. Health, 1987.

Warwick, Donald P., and Charles A, Lininger. *The Sample Survey: Theory and Practice.* New York: McGraw, 1975.

Watzman, Suzanne. "Principles of Effective Communication Design: A Tutorial." *Proceedings of the International Technical Communication Conference.* Washington, DC: Society for Technical Communication: 1988. 128-129.

Weisman, Herman M. *Basic Technical Writing,* 3rd ed. Columbus, Ohio: Charles E. Merrill, 1974.

While, Jan V. *Graphic Design for the Electronic Age.* New York: Watson-Guptill, 1988.

While, Jan. *Using Charts and Graphs.* New York: Bowker, 1984.

Williams, Joseph M. "How Can Functional Sentence Perspective Help Technical Writers Compose Readable Documents?" *Solving Problems in Technical Writing.* Ed. Lynn Beene and Peter While. New York: Oxford, 1988, 91--107.

Witte, Stephen. "Topical Structure and Revision: An Exploratory Study." *College Composition and Communication* 34.3 (1983), 313-341.

Wolcott, H.F. *Writing up qualitative research,* 2nd edn. London: Sage. 2001

Woods, P *Successful Writing for Qualitative Researchers.* London: RoutledgeFalmer.

Xerox Publishing Standards: *A Manual of Style and Design.* New York: Xerox Press, 1988.

Zinsser, William. *On Writing Well: An Informal Guide to Writing Nonfiction.* New York: Harper & Row, 1976.

# Index